I0441995

WITHOUT CONSENT

WITHOUT CONSENT

Without Intent

Valerie H Knowles Ph.D

ISBN: 1530871611
ISBN 13: 9781530871612
Library of Congress Control Number: 2016909703
CreateSpace Independent Publishing Platform
North Charleston, South Carolina

TABLE OF CONTENTS

Acknowledgements

Words cannot adequately express the depth of my gratitude for all of those persons who assisted me in completing my doctoral dissertation. My dissertation served as the foundation for this publication. These persons include the members of my initial Committees, Dr. William Green, Dr. Risper Awuor, Dr. Denton Rhone, Dr. Teran Milford (deceased), and Dr. Nicole Mauzard. Special appreciation is extended to those persons who guided me through the final stages to completion. These persons include Dr. Gloria Gregory, Dr. Vivienne Quarrie, Dr. Dave Higgins, and Dr. Marsha Pabarue. Miss Caddabra Bernard, thank you for your essential editorial assistance. Mrs. Shauna Sinclair, thank you for your professionalism and commitment to the doctoral program. Your assistance was invaluable. I am grateful to the Bahamas Ministry of Education and Technology, especially the school principals, guidance counselors and curriculum officers who made every effort to assist me. Thank you, Dr. Bonita Stanton, of the Focus on Youth Project, for your assistance. Nothing could have happened without the unwavering support of my family, most poignantly the support of my mother Mrs. Emerald Hepburn who over the many years insisted that incompletion was not an option. Thank you, Knijah Anu-bi, my daughter, for being the still, quiet voice that kept telling me that I could finish. To GOD be the glory in all things.

Introduction

Sexual Violence

Let It Rest (victim's narrative: a true story)

When my friends raped me, it did hurt me really bad.
Bleed, but didn't breed, angry, scared, shame, sad.
Didn't tell nobody either, didn't want dem call me "bad."
People always told me 'bout dem friends I use to have.
For a long time, had it on the shelf, nobody to blame,
$\qquad$ blamed me
$\qquad$ blamed myself.
But when my daddy raped me, seventh time, drunk
on da floor, i screamed in and outside me, Lord,
i can't take much more, what to do, he cried so hard
"Don't call da police baby" tears, cries, rum, please.
"Each time, I pray, God does forgive me, won't you
$\qquad$ forgive me too,
$\qquad$ forgive me, please?"
My family for true did have so much stress, i laid
my head on my pillow and let it rest till one girl at
school cross me and i open her arm with one deep
slice, fooled by hidden stress, i thought i had put my
hurt to bed, had taken the pain off my chest off
$\qquad$ my chest!!!
$\qquad$ My Chest.

Incarcerated, detained i thought i had it together
$\qquad$ i thought i had let it rest.

Valerie Knowles. *african children cry* (2016)[53]

Many believe they have heard all there is to hear on the topic of sexual violence. In the minds of others, only elitist women play the topic of sexual violence over and over again in an effort to earn more than their fair share of political attention. From the perspective of these persons, the topic should be laid to rest. However in my job as a child and adolescent psychologist, not a week went by without my meeting victims with stories like the one outlined in the above epigraph (Let It Rest). So while I did recognize that some persons were suffering from sexual-violence-fatigue as a subject matter, I chose to ignore that group of persons. I chose to publish the findings of my study on sexual violence and the associated thought patterns of selected school-leaving Bahamian adolescents.

My research focused on rape-myths, healthy-relationship myths, and sexual violence response efficacy. A rape-myth was defined as any statistically false belief about sexual violence, perpetrators, and victims that functioned to deny or justify sexual aggression. A healthy-relationship myth was defined as any statistically false belief about what constituted healthy intimate relationships. Research studies showed that there was a clear relationship between acceptance of rape myths and sexual assault[47]. These false beliefs could function to facilitate the use of violence within the relationship.[89] Sexual violence response efficacy was defined as being prepared to respond effectively in the face of victimization. My targeted group was selected Bahamian school- leavers.

The title of this book, *'Without Consent'* reflects the idea that through the socialization (child rearing) process, many children in the Caribbean are inadvertently being desensitized and mis-educated about the nature and consequences of sexual violence. Even when youth become legally able to consent there are many instances of uninformed consent, consent based on misinformation. The school system, despite its best efforts, has often been ineffective in uprooting some of the thought patterns supportive of sexual violence. Consequently, many youths leave school with a world view supportive of the process and notion of sexual victimization.

Without Consent gives insight into the parenting, socialization and formal-education factors that could have contributed to this reality. It presents victim narratives in poetic form to give real life examples of some of the issues presented. This publication includes recommendations to assist parents and school personnel to reduce the chances of Caribbean youths entering into adulthood with a cognitive framework that is insensitive to or ignorant of the pain and nuances of sexual violence.

1

SEXUAL VIOLENCE:
THE CARIBBEAN-BAHAMIAN CONTEXT

Le Franc and associates conducted a population-based study on sexual violence among adolescents and young adults in Barbados, Jamaica, and Trinidad.[61] Forty-eight percent of the sexually active females perceived their first sexual act as being forced. These statistics remain relevant to this date.[35] The United Nations Development Program's Caribbean Human Development Report (2012) noted that in the Caribbean, gender is the strongest predictor of criminal victimization.[104] The Bahamas is no different. Amid its structural prosperity and progress, the Bahamas was listed as having one the higher per capita rate of reported sexual violence in the world. [103, 79] The Inter-American Development Bank's report "Situation of Youth in the Bahamas" noted that as early as 1998, 45 percent the sexually active female adolescents and 13 percent of the active males had reported that their first sexual experience was forced.[11, 104] In another vein, more than being concerned about sexual violence in general, specific concern has been expressed about the younger age of victims and the growing number of group assaults. UNDOC (2012) noted that there were increasing numbers of underage victims across the Caribbean, and gang rapes were being more commonly reported.

In looking more closely at the Bahamas, the preceding paragraph noted that there has been a long standing concern about sexual violence. Another example of this was an informal study that was conducted 10 years ago. In my former capacity as manager of the Health and Family Life Resource Centre of the Bahamas Family Planning Association, there was an informal investigation of the ages of sexual initiation in a group of student mothers. At that time, of the 307 cases reviewed, 103 had their first sexual experience at the age of fifteen, eighty-nine at fourteen, forty-six at age thirteen, fourteen at age twelve, six at age eleven and one at age ten.[52] The implications for the prevalence of statutory rape were clear even at that point.

This premature sexualization through rape, sexual assault, molestation, and other acts of sexual violence can negatively impact development.

Dr. Sandra Dean Patterson a Bahamian social worker also reflected on the premature sexualization of Bahamian children. Dr. Sandra Dean-Patterson noted that there were certain factions within the Bahamian society that were quick to blame children for their sexualized behavior. Those blaming the children usually ignored the role that adults played in contributing to the victimization of these children. She suggested that the behavior people perceived as promiscuous or transactional, that is, girls selling or exchanging their bodies for gifts, was really symptomatic of sexual violation early in life. Dr. Patterson noted that the number of inappropriately sexualized children continues to increase.[74]

Dr. David Allen, a Bahamian psychiatrist noted what he termed as a normalization of behaviors that could be classified as prostitution. Girls in his research focus group who engaged in transactional sexual relationships with older partners were not concerned about using their bodies to attain material advantages. The girls did not perceive their behavior as prostitution. They called it survival. Transactional sex was part of their reality. Allen noted that some teenagers agreed that statutory rape was part of the "common culture" for a significant number of young persons. These transactional sexual liaisons began as early as age thirteen. Partners were typically between twenty and forty years old.[74]

Psychodynamic Realities

In addition to the information mentioned above, there is widespread misunderstanding about the diverse nature of sexual violence. Many erroneously associate sexual violence with pleasure or perceived it as a mild negative experience with minimal harm. There are persons who become immediately enraged when someone is suddenly and violently molested by an adult, but may not express the same outrage when there are statutory implications. There is not the understanding that molestation that occurs after a well-thought-out strategy involving persuasion, gift-giving, compliments, and ego-enhancing flattery by someone known and trusted by the perpetrator is still sexual violence. This recognition of the existence of this fallacy was one part of the motivation to study the thought patterns associated with sexual violence.

The Definition and Impact of Sexual Violence

Any sexual act that involves a non-consenting individual is an act of sexual violence. In such situations, the victim either does not consent, or lacks the ability to refuse or to prevent the act from occurring. Non-consenting individuals also include those persons giving consent but whose assent is made void by legal restrictions such as age and mental deficiency. Acts of sexual violence can range from:

(a) A completed nonconsensual sex act (i.e., rape)
(b) An attempted nonconsensual sex act
(c) Abusive sexual contact (e.g., unwanted touching)
(d) Noncontact sexual abuse, such as threatened sexual violence, ex-hibitionism, and verbal sexual harassment. [93, 20]

Sexual violence hurts psychologically and physically. It is important to stop looking only for blood stains on skirts and shorts. It is time to pay attention to the twisting of the victims' thoughts and emotions that are associated with the different forms of violence. The more we study sexual violence, the better equipped we become to reduce its harmful impact. There are several ways that children and adolescents are affected by sexual violence: [55, 6, and 21]

1. Betrayal Anger

The child can experience betrayal anger when the nature of their victim-ization becomes clear to them. The understanding that "the person who

I thought valued me and was protecting me, is the person who became comfortable violating me" may evoke feelings of anger, loss, worthlessness, and disillusionment and overwhelm the child. When the molestation continues for an extended period of time, the child may demonstrate signs of depression and denial, may feel mentally divorced from the reality of the violation, or may repress the memory. The child may demonstrate impaired judgment about the trustworthiness of others or the tendency to misinterpret the nature of other's behavior toward them. On becoming adults, the shadow of betrayal anger may form the motivation to continually initiate relationships with unstable or abusive partners so that the partners can behave in the expected disloyal manner.

2. Traumatic Sexualization

Children, who have been raped, molested or experienced sexual violence in any kind of way can come to view their bodies as objects, their greatest tool for negotiating business and interpersonal transactions. They may use sex to search for love and attachment. These are things that a child would ordinarily seek in a parent-child relationship. Consequently, when a child is traumatically sexualized, there is likely repetitive, precocious and inappropriate sexual behavior. Preschoolers may indulge in compulsive sex play. In adolescents, there may be patterns of multiple partnering to find love or in the execution of transactional sexual contracts (for money, recreation, gifts, or other tangible items). At a very young age, there is the premature exposure to the anxieties associated with potential unwanted pregnancy, sexually transmitted infections, abortions, and relationship violence.

3. Graphic Imagery Recall

Sometimes during molestation, victims absorb images of pain, force, humiliation, and a sense of loss of personal power and control. In addition to visual imagery, there are the psychological imaging issues.

These visual images of subjugation are combined with feelings of defeat, disloyalty, and betrayal. Flashbacks may be experienced. Given that children's self-image is influenced in part by the way others treat or respond to them, flashbacks can function as affirmations of worthlessness. "What kind of person must I be to warrant someone choosing to victimize me?" With each flashback this question may be asked and answered negatively.

4. Mind Bending

When children report molestation, the mental trauma of not being believed is sometimes as intense as the trauma of being believed. Being believed destroys families, friendships, and can result in the imprisonment of a valued family member or friend. This is a large burden to add to the ongoing trauma. The mind-bending trauma of an official investigation can be a source of further devastation. Psychological violation occurs when a child has to repeatedly sit through the experience of facing the perpetrator and being called a liar.

This is especially traumatic when the child knows that the molestation had occurred. The manipulative perpetrator's reconstruction of reality may suggest that the molestation never happened and that the child imagined it. When this mental-reconstruction technique is employed by someone the child has trusted, the experience is particularly devastating. The child may end up doubting his or her own sanity and his or her capacity to make sound judgments and good decisions. On occasion, the child will retract the accusation possibly because he or she now believes that the assault never really took place. All of the above experiences can enhance the child's vulnerability to being re-victimized.

5. Stigmatization

If victims of abuse come to perceive themselves as "ruined" or "spoiled" in some irreparable way, they may carry that stigma with them for a lifetime.

They may live experiencing a sense of "difference," understanding that something that has happened to them has not happened to other people. The sense of difference is reinforced by pressure for secrecy by family members. This call for secrecy could be a well-intentioned call made out of fear of what society will think of them if the molestation is discovered. Demeaning comments made by perpetrators during the course of molestation in an effort to secure secrecy compounds this aspect of the problem. The perpetrators' attempts to enforce secrecy usually involve having victims believe that they did something to bring the molestation upon themselves. For the victim to tell, this would mean telling on oneself.

6. Learned Helplessness

Upon evaluating the dynamics of molestation where the children initially fought psychologically or physically to ward off violation but were unsuccessful, they may believe that fighting off a predator or reporting the matter is forever useless because nothing can be done to stop the abuse. They perceive themselves as helpless in protecting themselves from harm because when they tried to defend themselves, they failed. They then stop trying to help or defend themselves in any situation.

7. Sexualization

For some female victims, her sense of worth becomes rooted in her sex appeal (I am nothing if I can't arouse men). No other skill, personality trait or characteristic becomes more important than her sex appeal. Energy goes into perfecting the art/science of gaining the attention of members of the opposite sex well beyond the level expected for others her age. To her, real power is reflected in the height of sexual frenzy that she can induce in a man. Her sense of self becomes objectified or made into a thing (I am *something* designed specifically for giving sexual pleasure). There is little appreciation for the personhood of the self. She has little appreciation for her gifts embedded in her intellectual, spiritual, social and emotional characteristics. Physical attractiveness is confused with sexy. Her standard of appropriate behavior is determined by whatever it is that she perceives men sexually prefer. To her it doesn't matter if the cheeks of her hips are showing as long as 'the men dem like it.'

Limitation of Impact

Not all children are impacted by victimization the same way. For children fourteen years old and younger, psychological distress was more acute when:

(a) It involved physical contact

(b) It included force

(c) It entailed anal or vaginal penetration

(d) It was inflicted by a known perpetrator

(e) The perpetrator was older than the victim by over four years

(f) The child was part of a dysfunctional family at the time of victimization

(g) The community blamed the child for the incident

(h) The victim accepted blame for the incident

(i) The victim perceived the molestation as the worst thing that could ever have happened to them

It is not unusual to hear persons say that a victim of sexual abuse has been ruined for life. While sexual violation can be emotionally devastating, devastation is not destiny. The power to aid in the healing of the child rests within the purview of all persons interacting with him or her and within the society as a whole. Your interaction with a victim, your behavior, and your words can either contribute to the child's further health or further distress. The negative psychological impact of child molestation will only last a lifetime if the public insists on it. Education to prevent and respond to sexual violence is crucial for making an impact on this societal challenge.

Reflections

Over the more than two decades of my career, witnessing the impact of violation in the professional context presented many painful but unique moments for reflection. Listed below are some these snapshots. These experiences are mentioned to highlight the necessity for continuing to advocate for community awareness of the influence of all forms of sexual violence, not just violent, stranger- based attacks. No matter how chronic the fatigue with the topic of sexual violence, reflecting on these encounters can function to motivate continued interests in sexual- violence risk reduction. Imagine:

- Meeting 12- 14 year olds who had been prematurely sexualized, objectified and or socialized to the point that they were determined to immediately become pregnant at all costs. They actively resisted efforts to help them prevent pregnancy.

- Meeting mothers who participated in the objectification of their children by insisting that their teenage daughters ask for rent money or other financial support from their boyfriends. Financial solvency was a prerequisite for parental approval of the relationship. The underlying philosophy was, 'What's the use of having a physical relationship, being sexually active if you cannot financially benefit from it?'

- Adults who aided and abetted the premature sexualization of children. These adults helped the children to flout parental attempts to discourage their illegal and or unhealthy liaisons. How did this happen? Someone living in the house would bring the youth home and introduce them to the head of the house as a friend. The offending adults allowed these children to sleep overnight or stay for extended periods in their homes without questioning them. Once the child's face became familiar to the head of the household and the child had gained resident status, this child would be allowed to have visits from friends. These friends would normally be friends that the parents did not approve off. Even if the head of the household did not approve of the relationship, these adults made no effort to contact the parents of the displaced children, or the guidance department of the children's schools or conduct some form of investigation about the children's predicament. If the resident child was able to contribute to the household in any way (cook, clean, wash, money) they were less likely to be encouraged to go back home.

- Parents who supported a statutory rape situation in their homes by reasoning that it was better for interaction to happen in their houses as opposed to having it happen in other, less safe places. Again if the situation benefited the household in any way, it was more likely to be tolerated.

- Meeting teenage males who had used trickery, deceit or some other form of psychological pressure to secure unprotected sex with their girlfriends, and who were now angry about the girls' family's decision to terminate a pregnancy that he had schemed to effect. Their anger at being thwarted contributed to a decision to be even more forceful or conniving the next time around.

- Meeting bright, intelligent, young women under the age of 18, who were prematurely sexualized to the point that they were willing to risk and lose everything to retain an illegal, highly prized, and sometimes physically abusive relationship. These were young ladies who despite having a higher than 2.00 grade point average, missed school, absented themselves from important examinations, forfeited free tutoring, gave up opportunities to travel, and even endured unpleasant disciplinary actions from their caregivers because of the way their value system was prioritized.

- Hearing the pain of young men who have been violated and who suffer not only the pain of violation but have now come to erroneously believe that their sexual orientation has been changed to something that is repulsive for them. Self- loathing overwhelms them.

- Reasoning with children to delay sexual involvement when they had been prematurely sexualized through a chronic exposure to pornography, and or they had had vicarious sexual experiences because of the exposure to sexual activities within their homes. A parent once commented, "I do not believe in hiding anything from my children. The more they know the better they will be able to deal with life. I don't hide my nakedness, screen movies, and tell them what they can or cannot listen to. They have to learn to deal with it because that is what real life is all about."

- Hearing young men talk about how they intend to 'swing' (deceive), then 'hold' (use friendly force), 'swell up' (impregnate) and then abandon some girl because the young lady rebuffed their advances. The comments would be made in jest but the violence implied is still unacceptable

Stories of Real Sexual Violence

Citation 1 below is a young lady's narrative of sexual harassment, "*Interview in Bed*. This is followed by "*I Need to Bleed*", a young lady's challenge with incest. A young lady's experience with prostitution, is noted in the citation "*Your Ho*." Sentiments on illegal transactional relationships are expressed in the 4th citation, "*My Baby Daddy Name*."

1. *Interview in Bed* *(sexual harassment: a real experience)*

Who will be hired today?

Sitting within polished office view,
waiting for my interview;
dressed for success,
graduations' best,
copies of degrees neatly
tucked in folder on my knees,
professionalism at ease;

In comes the boss,
distinguished head tossed,
with a calm 'good morning' bend,
when, a sad, old man,
key in hand, said, friend,
I will give you a hunch,
the only girl getting
hired today is:

the one who gives up
the boss man's 'lunch!'

2. I Need To Bleed (victim narrative of transactional incest: real story)

Please Lord let me bleed; I can't carry this seed within me.
There's no space for a little face among the dreams and
hopes mommy invested in me,

Mommy's life on hold, her sacrifices for me taking their toll,
I need to bleed, to have time to grow the seed for the better future
she willed, and planted in me.

Have mercy on my soul, this scared, fourteen years old,
I need courage not to hide the name of my Step Pappy.
my monthly bleed, for Mama please,

She thanks You every night for Step Pappy, she'll die if the seed
of his incestuous deed, grows uninterrupted nine months within me.
Let me bleed, please,
to hide his need for repayment for education, food and money.

2. Your Ho' *(teenager trapped in prostitution: real story)*

Listen how you name me; clothed, how you framed me
Busy at what you taught me; sitting where you left me
  My shoe, now heavy on your foot.

Firsthand knowledge, earning rent, sex didn't require legal consent.
Nakedness no longer needs the dark; no condom purchased for
my heart.
  My shoe, now heavy on your foot;

69 not always a number; ""sleep with" didn't always have slumber.
"Juicin" didn't always need fruit; didn't need all that pain in my youth.
  My shoe, now heavy on your foot

'Balls' not always with bat; sometimes raincoat without hat.
"Doggies" didn't all have fleas; there was no pleasure on my
knees
  My shoe, now heavy on your foot

Rape didn't always call police; sadly not only parents beat.
Pain, invisible, running deep; no discretion now with whom I "sleep"
  A mile, in my shoe now heavy on your feet.

Listen how you judge me! clothed in what you bought me.
Busy at what they pay me; sitting where they displaced me.
  A mile, in my shoe, now heavy on their foot.

Listen how they name you; hear them publicly defame you
But me I do blame you; Hope I publicly shame you
  For these shoes, now heavy on my foot

  Valerie Knowles african children cry, (2016)

4. *My Baby Daddy Name*
(teenager's proud reflection on statutory rape: true account)

He say don't tell you'll his name, you'll will try jailing him, giving him the blame.
Though he call me first, is me who gone to him, using my own mind and yes it's a sin.
Don't ask me again and no I ain't shame, I will not tell you, my baby daddy name.

He 34, he know my age, fourteen in couple a days, yes I go to his house out west.
Only out there, I could get some rest, home for me is cursing, poverty and pain yes he been to jail twice, I ain't shame, I still ain't tellin you'll my baby daddy name.

I know he married and yes, I ain't he wife, stay out my business Ms. and get ya own life.
He listens when I talk, yes he buy me things, but I have the man, and you have da rings. Yeah I use he cell, use he ATM too, but my baby daddy name gat nuttin ta do with you.

True Mam, I is number two, but from what I hear, wish I could say the same about you.
No attitude mam, tellin it like it is, this the way to play mam, take the Bahamian quiz. Who you know ain't have baby, don't takes dates, money and tings from man?

How much man with degree want be with a girl like me, least dis man tries to please me.
Who gat man with one woman, who gat a holy man, with manners and a savings plan?

Don't judge my good man, I know where he stand, half a you'll talkin gat she-he man

Remember he say don't tell you'll his name, you'll will try jail him, give him the blame.
Though he call me first, is me who gone to him, using my own mind, and yes it's a sin.
Don't ask me again and no I ain't shame, I will not tell you, my baby daddy name.

Valerie Knowles african children cry, (2016)

The above citations are all excerpts from the publication *african children cry*. The first edition was published in 2008, the second, 2016 edited version is in press.

2

I DON'T TEACH IT: SEXUAL VIOLENCE, TEACHERS, PEDAGOGY, AND CURRICULUM DEVELOPMENT

Deconstructing myths through curriculum exposure should reduce support for sexual violence. Effective intervention requires knowledge, activities and skills that uproot the strongly held beliefs that support sexual violence. Yet some teachers want nothing to do with any subject material involving the 's' (sex) word. In the Bahamas, the Health and Family Life Education (HFLE) curriculum is the avenue authorized by the Ministry of Education to deal directly with sexual and reproductive health, and with sexual violence. Topics related to sexual violence, sexual and reproductive health, and gender issues are all part of the written and intended curriculum. Research findings have indicated that many risk-reduction-curriculum-intervention programs can impact cognitions associated with sexual violence. [89, 90, 5].

Sustainable change in cognitions required extended exposure to curriculum intervention along with follow-up-reinforcement activities. If after 12 years students' educational experiences were not making a significant impact on deep, culturally embedded values supportive of sexual violence, then it could not be said that students were being adequately prepared for forming and maintaining healthy relationships free of sexual coercion. If these violence-supportive cognitions were not being modified, to what extent could we say that our students were really being educated?

At the time of my study two risk reduction curricula were being taught in the public school system. One curriculum was the traditional Health and Family Life Education (HFLE) curriculum. The other curriculum was the Focus on Youth – Caribbean curriculum. The HFLE curriculum like many other traditional curricula, was subject-based, focused on information, and used traditional teaching methods. *Application* of knowledge was not a top priority. The supplemental curriculum, the Focus on Youth–Caribbean curriculum (FOY-C) was a skills-based, student-centered, interactive curriculum that was introduced into the school system about thirteen years ago as a preventative initiative to reduce the incidences of HIV infection among young people. This FOY-C curriculum, though funded through an HIV initiative, promoted the acquisition of skills and knowledge that could be employed in any high risk decision making process. Curriculum activities included values and attitude-clarification exercises, skill development in conflict resolution, analyzing and forming responses to high-pressured communication, and analyzing the dynamics of peer pressure.

A twenty-four-month randomized follow-up assessment of the FOY-C curriculum showed that exposure to this risk-reduction curriculum positively impacted cognitive correlates of risky sexual behavior.[38] Why include the FOY-C, an HIV risk reduction initiative when the study was about sexual violence? Did the study compare apples with oranges? The FOY-C, as mentioned, was an HIV/AIDS-risk-reduction curriculum. What was the premise for assuming that this curriculum could impact selected cognitive variables associated with sexual violence? The World Health Organization (WHO) in conjunction with the Joint United Nations Programme on HIV/AIDS (UNAIDS) indicated that there was a clear etiological connection between HIV/AIDS and sexual violence.

Normative power imbalances, perceptual skews, myths, and social dislocations related to gender inequality influence vulnerability to HIV, and to sexual violence. The personal decisions to *accept* risky sexual behavior or *perpetrate* acts of sexual violence are all interconnected and tied to the same psychosocial variables. Given this shared etiology then, curriculum intervention that affected the cognitive correlates of behavior associated with HIV infection should also affect behavior associated with sexual violence. [33, 3] It was understood that curriculum intervention (whether by the FOY-C or the indigenous HFLE curriculum) that addressed the culturally embedded, gender-related norms and myths of the region should impact the cognitive correlates of violent sexual behavior.

The Challenge of Dosage: Teacher Fidelity of Implementation

Should we sit back and assume that teachers are teaching the assigned curriculum content on sexual violence risk reduction? Credible attributions of curriculum influence depend on the fidelity or faithfulness of teacher implementation. There are several forms of curriculum implementation. [105] There is:

(a) The <u>intended</u> curriculum (formal written document produced by relevant officials about what students should learn about sexual violence; this content may differ from the ideals espoused by the teachers developing the document)

(b) The <u>interpreted</u> curriculum (the content and concepts of sexual violence as understood by the class teacher)

(c) The <u>enacted</u> curriculum (the actual sexual violence risk reduction processes used by the teacher when teaching the content)

(d) The <u>experiential</u> curriculum (the content and processes as experienced by the students when being taught)

(e) The <u>assessed</u> curriculum (the sexual violence risk reduction processes and content measured by the school's assessment process)

(f) The <u>learned</u> curriculum (what students actually learned about sexual violence).

Despite the objectives of education administrators, there are times when teachers do not present the intended curriculum. Teachers may choose to neglect topics involving the word and concept of 'sex'. This is especially so for teachers who may be uncomfortable with an in-depth discussion or teaching of sexual and reproductive health and rights education topics (Knowles and others 2012).

Teacher Discomfort

There are teachers who experience discomfort talking about sexual violence when sexual violence is misunderstood to be a matter of "sexuality" as opposed to it being a matter involving "violence" and "exploitation." This group may be more comfortable talking about violence in general but not about sexual violence. Other teachers are more comfortable talking only about violent, physical rape by strangers, involving visible damage. They experience discomfort teaching about the other categories of sexual violence (incest, acquaintance, date, statutory, violations).

For some teachers, there is the perception that teaching sexual and reproductive rights and education goes against their Christian religious beliefs. Within their value base, sex outside of marriage is wrong. Any teaching in this content area even though it may be a health based prevention intervention is perceived as promoting sex outside of marriage. There are those teachers who believe that any reference to sex enhances curiosity about sex. This perceived curiosity is believed to be an impetus for increased experimentation. For this group of teachers open discussions about any topic connected with sex (whether violence is included or not) is perceived as violating the sacredness and mystery of sex. Sex was a topic reserved for married people.

Another reason that students may not be exposed to sexual violence risk reduction exercises is the diminished value given to Health and Family Life Education as a credible and useful subject. There are times that teachers use the time allotted to HFLE to cover other examinable topics that may have been missed during the course of a busy week (Knowles and others 2012). In addition, a Caribbean assessment of teacher integration of HFLE into the normal teacher schedule showed that only 30 percent of the teachers were able to fully accommodate a mandated HFLE curriculum.[109]

> Despite enthusiasm, teachers expressed concerns throughout the study about whether there was enough time to complete lessons. Teachers had ongoing problems with scheduling HFLE class time, disruptions in school scheduling, and time management challenges. The concern was whether sufficient time is *ever* allocated for HFLE (or can be allotted, given other teaching priorities and the *many* school events and activities). In addition to the meager time allotments, low curriculum priority, many teachers had little classroom experience or any experience at all using the interactive strategies of the more effective pedagogy associated with effective health and family life education curricula. [108,109]

Can we expect change if a significant number of teachers choose not to or are unable to teach the content? Given the strength of strong cultural influences on cognitions of sexual violence, little impact can be made if at school cognitions are not consistently challenged in a sequential manner. The right pedagogy is needed in the right dosage if there is to be a significant deconstruction of the cognitions supportive of sexual violence. The results of my study indicated that there were statistically significant differences between children who had been systematically exposed to a structured risk reduction curriculum when compared to children whose teachers only exposed them to the HFLE or risk reduction content on an ad hoc basis. There were differences in the number of rape myths accepted, the number of healthy-relationship myths accepted, and differences in the levels of response efficacy. Students exposed to the more structured risk reduction curricula accepted lower numbers of rape myth, healthy-relationship myths.

Curriculum Intervention

In examining curriculum impact on cognitions supportive of sexual violence, my study examined the influence of deliberate education interventions on students' knowledge base and perceptual schema as they related to sexual violence. Students who participated in the study completed questionnaires about sexual violence at the end of the 12th grade. Through the process of randomization students were exposed to one of two different risk reduction curricula in the 10th Grade. As mentioned at the beginning of this chapter, one of the risk-reduction curricula used in this study was the indigenous secondary school Health and Family Life Education (HFLE) curriculum. This curriculum was scheduled as a normal part of the secondary-school timetable. Some students were exposed to the Focus on Youth–Caribbean (FOY-C) risk-reduction curriculum. This curriculum as mentioned earlier was an American-based curriculum that was adapted for implementation in the Bahamian school system as a risk-reduction tool. Students who received the FOY-C curriculum were given two booster sessions during the 11th grade. Booster sessions allowed for a review of the concepts covered. Questionnaires were administered to all participants during the national Bahamas General Certificate of Secondary Education (BGCS) examination period.

Reflections: Sexual Violence, Teachers, Pedagogy, and Curriculum Development

Most teachers are hard workers. There may be many jobs that allow persons to idle all day and do no work. Teaching is not one of them. It is virtually impossible to sit in the front of 30 children, do nothing and not have chaos. So to avoid this level of burnout even the most demotivated teacher will make an effort to engage the students sitting in the front of them. Self- preservation demands it. Therefore no comment made here is meant to undermine any persons in this noble profession.

Having said that, I need to say that I found it hard to understand the discomfort of some teachers for the teaching of sexual and reproductive health education. This discomfort extended to the topic of sexual violence risk reduction education. This discomfort remained even though the Ministry of Education had assigned and approved these topics for the Health and Family Life Education curriculum. I agree that topics involving sexual and reproductive health and rights are not easy to deliver. Strength was needed to retain composure while ill-formed persons assumed the worst about my character. Some assumed that if I could use words like vagina, anus and penis so openly that I must be living a debauched lifestyle. On one occasion I was accused of 'desecrating the babies' of the nation for suggesting that students should know the proper names of their private parts and understand the dynamics of reproduction before they entered high school. Others challenged my right to call myself Christian given my advocacy in this area. At the extreme end some persons made a connection between teaching sexual violence risk reduction and the support of extreme feminism. The greatest resistance did not come from parents.

In a developing country that wrestles with HIV/AIDS, unwanted teenage pregnancies, teen violence, inadequate parenting, male-student attrition, truancy, non-communicable diseases, and academic underachievement, how is it irrelevant to teach HFLE which includes the topic of sexual violence risk reduction? Why is a course irrelevant when it encourages the open discussion of adolescent stress management techniques, health and wellness, food choices, nutrition, ethics, coping with peer pressure, enhancing positive decision making skills, conflict resolutions skills, preventing pregnancy and sexually transmitted infections, constructive gender relations, drug abuse prevention, goal setting, sexual violence risk reduction and prevention etc. Even more interesting is the teacher-based discomfort associated with discussing any issue related to sexual and reproductive health and rights education. Listed below are some memorable and concerning events that emerged from my experiences before, during and after my research:

- Meeting graduating grade 6 students, ready to transition to high school who, in addition to not knowing the proper names of their private parts, had no idea of what puberty was, the power of hormones or how their lives were going to be impacted by this stage of development.

- Talking to high school students who practiced oral and anal sex but who did not think they were sexually active and did not connect violation with these parts of their bodies

- Meeting high school students who were comfortable having had more sexual experience than they could count on their two hands. They sensed no moral, physical, emotional, legal limits to their behaviour. Violation was a term that they used loosely

- Meeting male students who believed in their right to hit and possess and female students who accepted the right to be hit and possessed. This was so even if the relationship lasted only two weeks.

- Meeting the above mentioned teachers who were resistant to teaching primary school children the proper names for their private body parts. Penis and vagina were taboo words. The teachers themselves would not say the words in a conversation with me.

- Meeting teachers who were prepared to and did skip over reproduction, sexual violence and related health topics.

- Experiencing principals who scratched Health and Family Life Education off teachers' submitted timetables

- Responding to principals who said the discussion of private parts and sexual and reproductive health will never take place in their schools. It was the parents' job.

- Having educational officials who believed advocacy was vulgar. Being referred to as vulgar was one of the toughest experience of a life-long career.

- Meeting HFLE teachers, with degrees in the area, who had been specifically trained to teach sexual and reproductive health education but were uncomfortable talking about sexual violence in its many facets. Many of them were afraid of parental responses.

- Conversing with teachers who insisted that they should teach about the digestive system, the respiratory system and every other system except the reproductive system because it was the parents' job to teach this topic.

Power

In contrast it was empowering to interact with many teachers and principals who were advocates for the holism that Health and Family Life Education brings to the timetable. During the research period, the Senior Education Officer for Health and Family Life Education in the Ministry of Education Science and Technology Mrs. Glenda Rolle, (along with Mrs. Sabrina Skinner, Superintendents Helen Simmons Johnson, Dr. Lenora Black and Assistant Director of Education Ms. Verona Seymour) tirelessly supported administrative efforts to integrate risk reduction curricula into the public education system. Their efforts were bolstered by the work of Mrs. Lynette Deveaux and Dr. Sonia Lunn of the Ministry of Health's risk reduction initiatives. These persons supported the systematic integration of risk reduction curricula into the timetable inclusive of the topic of sexual violence. At the same time, it was encouraging to meet thousands of students who were committed to avoiding risky lifestyles. These were students who came to school focused on maximizing their learning opportunities and ably resisted the pressure to do otherwise.

3

CULTURAL FOUNDATIONS: BUILDING THOUGHT PATTERNS SUPPORTIVE OF SEXUAL VIOLENCE

Cognitions, thought patterns about victims and violence, myths, and healthy relationships are learned through the gender-socialization (child rearing) process. Within the framework of social learning theory, learning can occur by direct instruction, and or through imitative, vicarious, or observational methods [49, 68]. In reference to the gender-socialization process, "gender" can be defined as the widely shared and taught expectations and norms about what are appropriate male and female behaviors, responsibilities, characteristics, and roles.[42] Although learning never ceases, it is during the formative years that persons attain their early perceptual framework for interpreting behavioral cues around them.

Very early in life we learn to interpret behaviour, to form opinions about what it means if a woman or man says this or that, or does this or that. A review of the literature and anecdotal experience identified some of the social lessons learned that could be associated with sexual violence. These message-statements outlined below may be uttered directly by parents and significant others with no malicious intent. However whether the intent is malicious or not the thoughts are transmitted nonetheless.

CULTURAL MESSAGE-STATEMENTS SUPPORTIVE OF SEXUAL VIOLENCE

Message 1: If you do not want to be violated, then behave like a lady.

How many times have you heard this statement or said it yourself? The framework for this thought pattern is rooted in the constructs of "marianismo" and "machismo". These are the Latin American and Caribbean's ideals or perceptual molds that shape our regional forms of femininity and masculinity and the prescribed relationships between them. [41] Marianismo arises through Judeo Christian religious influences in the culture. Religion is entrenched in the lives of Caribbean people. [46] In a strongly religious setting, the ideal Christian feminine persona is cast in the role and psyche of the Virgin Mary (Madonna). Marianismo suggests that the feminine ideal, the proper way for a woman to behave is to be chaste, virginal, subordinate, obedient, morally superior, and spiritually grounded. [36,42, 48] It is the socially prescribed ideal for which women should strive. Many of the rape and sexual violence relationships-myths, and related thought patterns have been influenced by this feminine ideal.

Persons who have assimilated this ideal are more likely to show responses to victimization that blame the victim for their predicament. For example in the case of female victims thinking that the victim was at fault because she was behaving in an unbecoming of a good women, a provocative manner, or she was frequenting a place women were not supposed to be in. Any violence she experiences is her fault for not being or behaving as the good woman. These are not new thoughts. Lonsway and Fitzgerald as early as 1994 noted that women acting outside of the cultural ideal made themselves vulnerable to cultural reprimand.

Rape-myth Acceptance

Early studies of incarcerated offenders found a strong presence of cognitions, thought patterns that rationalized, and justified sexual violence [88]. It was important to understand the structure and function of myths as an element of the thought patterns of violators. We could only study thought patterns because it is not ethical or possible to study the perpetrator in the act of committing a sexual offense.

Schwendinger and Schwendinger (1974) and Brownmiller (1975) uncovered the existence and influence of rape myths and brought this discovery into the discourse on sexual violence. Burt (as cited in Iconis 2008) had defined rape-myths as prejudicial, culturally supported, stereotyped, false beliefs about rape, rape victims, and rapists that functioned to sustain sexual violence by blaming the victim and exonerating the perpetrators. Rape myths were persistently believed even in the face of evidence proving their falsity.[63] Theories that conceptualized acts of sexual violence as being driven by uncontrolled sexual passion blamed the women or the victims for being victimized. From this perspective, sexual violence would not occur if women behaved in a manner that would not excite the sexual passions of males.

What are some of the rape-myths and how do these myths justify the perpetrator of sexual violence? The more popular myths suggest that on the average victims, male or female either:

(a) Ask for the rape or sexual violence
(b) Have a different definition of sexual violence from that of the perpetrator because from the perpetrator's perspective there was nothing wrong with what happened, what happened was not really rape
(c) Misunderstand the intention of the perpetrator who did not mean it to be rape

(d) <u>Misunderstand their own intentions</u> because they did indeed want the sexual activity

(e) <u>Lie</u>; if the victim is female, she is deliberately slandering the perpetrator's name and <u>perpetrating a fraud</u> against him

(f) Exaggerate; <u>is exaggerating the impact</u> that the violation has had on him/her.
No real harm was experienced because sexual violence is a small, trivial thing

(g) Delusional: because there is a big chance that no violence occurred as rape or sexual violence is not a normative event, it <u>is a rare phenomenon.</u>[91]

Myths in the Region

One of the most strongly rooted myths or thought patterns in the Latin American and Caribbean (LAC) region is that the way women dress and behave can provoke men to sexual violence.[27] Associated with this myth is the idea that women, by their dress, are asking to be violated in one form or the other. A study in Peru found that young men believed that forced sex was justifiable if the victims were perceived to be flirting and then in turn denied or unfairly rejected offers for sex. Amnesty International in a survey in Jamaica found that 66 percent of men and 49 percent of women agreed with the idea that women and girls sometimes brought rape upon themselves. It also pointed out that children shared these beliefs, which indicated that some of these myths were transferred very early in the socialization process.[4, 95]

Another myth is that men have uncontrollable sexual desires. Restraint is acceptable for women but not for a man. One research study revealed that many women in Brazil believed that men needed sex and that men would be driven to abuse or perceived themselves as having been abandoned if they did not have it. [27] It was also found that communities that placed a high premium on female virginity at the time of marriage, women and girls who may have experienced any form of willing premarital sex were not likely to be considered to be genuine rape victims.[27] In other studies it was noted that victims' sexual histories impacted the perception of their claims of being violated. Coerced penetration was more likely to be considered an offense if the victim was a perceived virgin. When victims were not virgins, many young men failed to support the allegation of rape because it was difficult to believe that they were forced.[91] Damage was to be assessed in relation to the victim's sexual history. The perception was that an attack had consequences similar to a casual sexual encounter especially if the attacker was a long-term partner as opposed to a stranger. Middle-aged to older generations of persons within the Latin America and Caribbean region hold these beliefs more strongly. In the more modernized societies of today, however, younger men and women within the region show less cognitive support for sexual violence [27]. An important dynamic here is that sexual violence myths are highly resistant to change. They are persistently believed even when they have little empirical basis in reality.

Message 2: If you do not want to be violated, then do not dress like a Jezebel.

Again, the perpetrator is not responsible. In contrast to the Madonna ideal is the Jezebel ideal. According to Olive (2012), the symbolic female Jezebel is conniving, sexually promiscuous, lustful, and immoral. She can hardly be violated sexually. A careful scrutiny of rape and healthy-relationship mythology will show an infusion of the Jezebel--Madonna influence. Sexual violence is understood depending on how the victim was dressed that is, whether she dressed and behaved like the symbolic Jezebel. The Jezebel-dress would be very revealing. Make-up would be gaudy and color- scheme fluorescent. The whole ensemble would be shouting out for attention. Acceptance of this ideal with the associated stereotypes facilitates myth acceptance.

Acceptance of this myth and ideal also contributes to poor response efficacy. When victimized and having to disclose or confront their sexual assaults, female victims can inadvertently find themselves resolving the dilemma of these two different stereotypes: Jezebel and Madonna. [77] There are negative consequences on either side of the dilemma. Rape, sexual violence myth acceptance allows a woman's dress, her behavior, her sexual history, and her relationship with the predator to influence the credibility of her consent. If she is assessed as Jezebel, the victim may find that persons may believe that no real assault happened. [70] If assessed as a Madonna, her perceived purity is ruined. Any gendered environment that formally sanctions only two options for good women (marriage or abstinence) could fuel silence in response to victimization. Some victims may feel compelled to remain silent if they perceive their violation as having destroyed their purity. Silence helps them preserve their social image of purity.

Paradoxically though, women of African-descent have always had a dilemma with the Marianismo-Jezebel dialectic. In the same way that the ideal of the Virgin Mary assumed feminine purity, Judeo Christian's Jezebel ideal assumed feminine harlotry, always ready for sex even if it involved violence. Unfortunately, the history of the woman of African-descent presented her in stark contrast to the Madonna ideal. Donovan and Williams (as cited in Olive 2012) noted that:

> …black women were subjected to forced breeding and rape. When laws prohibited the importation of Africans, black women were required to reproduce children for the depleted slave work force. These acts were committed by slave owners and enslaved men. (p. 1)

This experience of institutionalized, legitimate sexual violence followed female slaves wherever they were kept in bondage, be it in America or in the Bahamas. Theirs was not always a history of consensual liaisons or Madonna privilege. Theirs was a vulnerability of never being believed when social elements invoked the Jezebel branding.

Message 3: Married or single; a real man must be *known* to be sexually active.

It is interesting to note that there is no corresponding Jezebel persona for men. The male ideal, machismo, in contrast to the chastity of marianismo reflects virility, physical strength, sexual prowess, and aggression. Males are sometimes socialized into assertive hypersexuality as an important masculine construct. When raised in an environment where machismo is dominant and sexual prowess is valued, men are more likely to accept rape myths (she wants it, no harm done, it is a trivial matter). They are more likely to engage in risky or coercive sexual behavior as they respond to the pressure to establish their masculinity. See the sentiments (**Be a Man Boy:** A boy's experienced pressure to be deviant: a true account).

Be a Man Boy

Burst da nigga, boy! Show him you aint no punk!
Chap him boy, stab him, and burst him in the mouth.
Dat nigga dissin your ma boy! dese niggas take you for light.
Doon let niggas punk you boy, pick up dat knife and fight.

Gata get respect boy, doon let niggas take ya stripe!
You need to force down da girl boy, hurry break her in.
She braggin here bout she a virgin, force the ting in ma boy.
You need to get it right, you mussy like man hey, Mr. Polite.

If she say "no" boy, she dissin you, callin ya light, break in your girlfriend boy, I is ya Pa. I learnin you about ya rights!
Break down da jail cell boy, rape charge can't keep you in.
Bribe someone boy, find one a ya street brethren!

Burst one a dem prisoner' boy, so dey could see you een light.
Don't bend over for no break-in boy, know ya prisoner's rights
Chap the walls away boy, chapter quietly every night
Burst dem mental chains boy, for generations, holdin' you tight.

(Valerie Knowles african children cry, 2016)

Men acting outside of the machismo or hypermasculinity paradigms risk being socially devalued and labeled effeminate.

Message 4: She is supposed to say no; it's part of the mating game.'

For some there is the understanding that when a woman says no, she usually does not mean it. Myth acceptance (she really wants it, no real harm is done, it is a trivial thing) in this context fuels the potential for sexual violence. In desperation to meet socially prescribed criteria for masculinity and earn peer approval, some men may seek to attain sexual experience at any cost. They may ignore consent issues in an effort to secure their reputation (Thompson, Swartout, and Moss 2013). Myth acceptance helps them to justify their behavior.

Traditional religious beliefs about sex roles correlate positively with the acceptance of rape myths.[71] This is noted in instances where Holy Writings are interpreted in a manner that justifies aggression against women. Sexism facilitates sexual violence. Persons who accept rape-myth tend also to accept gender biases.[22, 66] Consumers of pornographic movies and magazines were more likely to accept rape myths.[50] This was so for both men and women. Acceptance and perception of interpersonal violence as a legitimate form of behavior also correlated positively with rape-myth acceptance.[12]

Message 5: Never let it be said that you can't keep a man.

It has been said that to be known as someone who cannot attract or keep a man is a very unflattering descriptor. [73] A woman who believes this message may demonstrate poor response efficacy when experiencing relationship challenges. Females who have been socialized to accept the machismo definition of masculinity (real men are hypersexual) and those who have internalized relationship and sexual violence myths (I aroused him to the point that he cannot control himself, it is because he loves me so much that he is so possessive) may be more inclined to overlook sexual aggression. Believing the myth that sexual violence is a natural part of a man's nature, some women may be reluctant to leave an unhealthy relationship and search for a safer one thinking there are too few men out there to risk losing the one they have. They tolerate sexual violence in their partner because from a myth-based perspective, having a bad man may be better than having no man at all.

Women may tolerate sexual aggression because of the fear of the marianismo backlash which may label them as promiscuous. This dilemma would be especially challenging for those taught that a good woman had only one man during her lifetime, that relationships were made in heaven, and that God sent her that abusive man as a gift. Marianismo would support her accepting the situation. There would be the fear of stigmatization if leaving a 'good' violent man and finding another man resulted in her going beyond the socially approved number of men that she was supposed to have. If she reasoned that male sexual aggression was natural, she would more than likely believe that irrespective of which man she ended up with, the result would be the same, sexual violence. After all, she would be expected to understand, 'that's how man go', so deal with it.

Healthy-relationship Myths

Healthy-relationship myths are statistically false beliefs or thought patterns about what constitutes healthy-dating behaviors.[87] An individual's perception of what constitutes a healthy relationship influences which behaviors will be tolerated in the dating relationship. Therefore, deconstructing these myths or thinking patterns should also reduce the incidents of sexual violence. Saedi pointed out three of the many romantic myths: (a) there are matches made in heaven; (b) after finding Mr. or Miss Right, it was important to stay connected to him or her at all costs, even in the face of suffering harm; and (c) love conquers all including the most blatant incompatibilities and destructive behavior. Another popular healthy-relationship myth is that possessiveness and extreme jealousy are signs of love and intimacy.

Acceptance of healthy-relationship myths can function as one of the cognitive vehicles that allow for the rationalization of sexual violence. In reality, these relationship attributes can be considered as precursors for violent behaviors. Relationships that do not allow for respect for personal space or privacy are not healthy. People in healthy relationships mutually recognize and respect their partners' family, friends, and other influencers.[45] When these aspects of a relationship are dysfunctional, there is a greater vulnerability for experiencing and accepting violence of any type, sexual violence included. Tolerance of violence or oppression in any aspect of a relationship can set the foundation for experiencing sexual violence.[43, 40]

Many of the risks factors associated with violence in intimate relationships were associated with beliefs or thoughts about the transactional elements of dating relationships. [70] Transactional elements involved issues about entitlement. Entitlement involved what privileges a person felt entitled to receive if they were the ones paying the greater costs for the date (what am I entitled to if I am the one who did the approaching or if I were the one approached, what am I entitled to if the date is at my place, what am I entitled to if we are driving in my car). Myths in any of these areas functioned as risk factors for sexual aggression. [25, 14]

Another relationship myth mentioned in research is the thought if someone has had sexual contact with an individual before then their refusal of a subsequent advance cannot be fully legitimate. College students in general and sexually aggressive men in particular believed that sexual precedence (a history of sexual intercourse) reduced the legitimacy of sexual refusal.[86] The myth here is that if a person is not a virgin, or if they have engaged in consenting sexual activity with the aggressor before, then there can be no legitimate refusal to sexual activity.

Message 6 "Nobody will want you if..."

In the same way that some of our patterns of verbal conflict reflect unhealthy violence in sexualization, so do some of the patterns of parental verbal discipline.

Some parents or significant others in their counseling efforts tie a child's self-worth to sex appeal:

"Try fix yourself up, how you expect to get a man lookin' like that."
"If you don't do this or that, you think any woman or man will want you?"
"No man want no smart woman, or fat woman, dumb woman, or skinny woman." 'How you expect to keep a man if..."

What is the message being delivered in the quotes above? Fix up yourself, go to school, set your goals in life, make decisions not for what will give you a sense of personal pride but for what will make you more sexually attractive to members of the opposite sex. The opinion of the opposite sex is presented as the most important factor in decision making. Again in the above instances, self-worth and internal motivation are tied to the power of sexual attraction. What are the chances that somebody with this mindset would choose to not tolerate sexual violence in a relationship?

Reflections on Sexual Violence and Cultural Support

These reflections focus on incidences or snapshots of cultural transmission of values and behaviour supportive of sexual violence. It has been my observation (Knowles 2008) that our children are inadvertently taught a similar message of gender imbalance and sexual violence as they listen to the way some adult women verbally resolve their conflicts. A good quarrel starts first with attacks on the opponent's natural negroid features. Derogatory references are made to her black skin with her "nappy head, big, broad nose, and her 'drop down, big lips." If the denigration of her negroid features does not subdue her, it then becomes necessary to go below the waist and make derogatory references to her private parts: "her wide dis' and slack "at," "her bust up" this and "dig out" that. All of these references are meant to insult the opponent by accusing her of having genitalia devalued by her chronic promiscuity.

If the woman remains petulant at this stage, then it becomes necessary to strike a near death blow. This is done by verbally attacking the sexual characteristics of the opponent's momma. References are made about "her mama deep dis" and "her mama wide dat." For a death blow, the fidelity of the woman's partner is attacked with 'your husband or boyfriend' desires me more than you. The conflict is only considered resolved when one party has completely obliterated the sexuality of the other through the desecration of the other's primary and secondary sexual characteristics. The effectiveness of this sexual cannibalism reflects a mind-set primed for victim blaming and shaming.

In a similar vein, there are some parents or significant others who during the course of discipline have called down or predicted victimization on their daughters as a consequence for some offending behavior. This is noted in comments like "you're such a slut, you need to get rape!" Some label their daughters, "bitches," "hos," and "sluts" long before the youth know what the words really mean. Sometimes the sexual innuendo is totally inappropriate. See the expression '*Raisin Leg*' outlined below. Self-definition by significant others can become a self-filling prophecy.

Raisin Leg (true incident of a young lady insulted by a neighbour who didn't like her clothes attributed her dress to sexual motives)

> "*Lil girl go home and cover up ya hip,*
> *put on underwear, and sew up that split,*
> *stand up straight to hide ya crease,*
> *everywhere you sit you leaving streak.*
> *Jelly, raisin thighs, rubbing, giving off heat,*
> *you scratchin in public like you gat flea*
> *It really hard for people to tell,*
> *if ya trying to catch man or you tryin to sell.*
> *With the bait you using, the most you ga see,*
> *is a left over beating and full HIV.*"

My experience has also brought me into contact with female students who believed that it was a game to "take somebody's man." It was a privilege and a boast to say that, 'my body, my skills could take your man." It was not a matter of the man choosing to go with them. It was their perception that once they began the seduction process, he could not help himself. Controlling his arousal was beyond his mental capacity. In the process, it was understood that one male in the seduction process could have multiple sexual experiences as each girl vied for the win. The chosen girl becomes the winner. She remains the winner subject to challenge by any other brave girl who wants to try to dethrone her. Both the successful and the unsuccessful contenders risk being beaten by each other for their efforts. The male remains the perceived passive element in this dynamic. In an era past, this behaviour may have been noticed at a more subtle level among adults. However it appears to have become a form of time consuming recreation within certain groups of students.

Another reality worthy of reflection is the insidious predatory nature of some adults. The predatory behaviour that we see today is not new. Decades ago, I personally experienced and witnessed this continuous harassing behaviour all around me. Harassment was present from adults as I walked home from school, from men sitting men on the walls, men working in the stores, at the gas stations, men with responsibility in church, youth group leaders, on summer jobs etc. As I reflect on those years, the attraction could not have been a physical attraction. Nothing about my physical characteristics was ever outstanding. The attraction appeared to be the air of apparent vulnerability.

My parents believed in community involvement and encouraged me to participate in as many educational and positive activities as possible. My parents trusted me and reality at times dictated that I went alone or with like-minded peers. Some assumed at times that the unaccompanied girls from 'over the hill' (inner city), those who were without transportation were fair game for exploitation. The stereotype was that there would be minimal if any resistance to unsolicited and illegal advances. After all we were only 'gyals from over the hill'. On more than one occasion, physical resistance was required on my part. One youth group leader almost lost an arm, a friend of the family almost lost sight in one eye and the bus driver of the youth group who suddenly couldn't find my address was awakened to the light with my threatening to maim him and then jump out of the window of the moving bus.

This resistance was needed in circumstances that were supposed to be the safest for young people at that time. Parents gave permission for their children to attend youth group functions at church. They encouraged their children to attend leadership training seminars, speech contests and other events with community service volunteer groups. They would never have assumed that predators lurked in those environments. Again it was not the predator with the gun and knife that posed the problem. It was the respectable adult in a position of authority wearing a smile, boasting a prestigious title and offering a friendly ride home who posed the problem. This was decades ago, imagine the challenge now.

My protection was that from an early age I had been warned and trained to respond when approached inappropriately. Secondly I had been taught that certain behaviours were outright wrong/ inappropriate. These behaviours remained wrong no matter how the person smiled when guiding you in that direction. Some of my peers were not so fortunate. They became pregnant, statutory rape victims. I have the poignant memory of my first and best childhood friend from my primary school days. The both of us won scholarships for high school at age 11, the first in our families and in our primary school to do so. She had to discontinue her academic quests when she became pregnant about three years later. Our lives dramatically and quickly changed, turning in different directions. It was difficult back then as a 13yr. old to understand all of the sociocultural forces impacting upon my friend's life. In my mind the only question I had was, 'Why did she not say no?' I blamed the victim. That experience was one of the forces that shaped my career interests from that time forward. Today I still bear a great deal of professional empathy for young people caught in similar situations.

In today's milieu, there are many young people who are still disgusted by the continual harassment for sexual favours. There are some that consider the harassment to be a normal part of the culture. Others do not consider the begging for favours as harassment. They are flattered by the attention. This dichotomy in perception was recently made clearer to me during a training presentation that I conducted for a group of grade 11 students. As a part of the training activities, there was an item that asked students to become aware of sexual harassment antics when going on job interviews, or job-seeking of any kind. Interestingly, there were some students who were not quite sure that there was anything wrong with being asked to exchange sexual favours for job opportunities.

This group felt that the task should ask them to assess risks and losses if they chose to take a chance on doing an exchange. This approach was perceived to be more realistic than to suggest that a request for an exchange was automatically out of the question. It was not fair to arbitrarily classify the exchange as morally wrong even though it was illegal. Questions included, 'What if the boss were rich, drove a nice car, offered large sums of money as gifts even if the job was not awarded? What if the boss-lady was pretty? What would male friends say if they found out I was propositioned by a female boss and turned her down?' This experience was reminiscent of the time when a group of students suggested that I seek professional help because I suggested that intimacy does not require an exchange of money. There were many other examples of the embedded support for violence that exceed the scope of this book. Suffice it to say there is much work to be done to begin to challenge and uproot these cognitions. The following chapter reviews the quantitative results of my study.

4

RAPE-MYTH ACCEPTANCE, HEALTHY-RELATIONSHIP-MYTH ACCEPTANCE, AND RESPONSE EFFICACY AMONG SCHOOL-LEAVING BAHAMIAN ADOLESCENTS

Of the more than 300 students who completed questionnaires that assessed their beliefs about aspects of sexual violence, 92 percent of them had summary scores that indicated a high risk for supporting sexual violence. Only 8 percent had summary scores that fell in the protected category. Those in the protected category had summary scores that indicated an unlikely support for sexual violence. In general, there were high levels of rape-myth acceptance, high levels of healthy-relationship-myth acceptance, and low average levels of response efficacy.

Question: **What levels of rape-myth acceptance existed among the selected graduating students?**

Rape-Myth Acceptance: Individual Responses

The majority of the more than 300 students 68% (211 students) were classified in one of the high-rape-myth-acceptor groups. What were these groupings?

- Group 1   Average to High Acceptors. These were participants accepting or not rejecting 8 to 10 of the eighteen myths presented. Thirty-four percent (105) of the participants' scores fell in this category.

- Group 2   Very High Rape-myth Acceptors. These were those who accepted or did not reject 11 or more of the 18 myths presented. Thirty-four percent (106) of the participants' scores fell into the very-high-acceptance category.

Part A
Sample of Myths Accepted by 50% or more Participants

- A woman who dresses in skimpy clothes should not be surprised if a man tries to force her to have sex.

  Thinking   : She wanted it.
  Function of this myth   : Blame the Victim.
  Accepted by   : 76% or 234 participants

- Men don't usually intend to force sex on a woman, but sometimes they "run hot" and get carried away.

  Thinking   : He didn't mean to do it.
  Function   : Excuse the Perpetrator.
  Accepted by   : 75% or 232 participants

- Rape happens when a man's sex drive goes out of control. (Men cannot control their sexual urges)

  Thinking   : He didn't mean to do it.
  Function of Myth   : Excuse the perpetrator.
  Accepted by   : 72% or 223 participants

- A lot of women lead a man on and then they cry rape.

  Thinking   : She lied.
  Function of Myth   : Blame the victim.
  Accepted by   : 72% or 221 participants

- Women tend to exaggerate how much rape affects them

  Thinking   : It's no big deal.

  Function   : Trivialize the event.

  Accepted by   : 58% or 179 participants

- Rape accusations are often used as a way of getting back at men.

  Thinking   : She lied.

  Function of Myth : Trivialize the event.

  Accepted by   : 58% or 180 participants

- When women are raped, it's often because the way they said no was unclear

  Thinking   : She asked for it.

  Function   : Excuse the perpetrator

  Accepted by   : 50% or 154 participants

- A woman who "teases" men or "plays with their minds" deserves anything that might happen

  Thinking   : She asked for it.

  Function   : Blame the victim.

  Accepted by   : 50% or 155 participants

- A woman who is raped while she is drunk is at least somewhat responsible for what happened to her

  Thinking   : She asked for it.

  Function   : Blame the victim.

  Accepted by   : 50% or 153 participants

Part B
Sample of Myths Accepted by less than 50% of Participants

- If a woman is willing to let a man touch her intimately and kiss her, then it's no big deal if he goes a little further and has sex with her.

   Thinking   : She asked for it.
   Function   : Blame the victim.
   Accepted by   : 47% or 146 participants

- If a woman doesn't fight back, you can't really say that it was rape.

   Thinking   : It wasn't really rape t.
   Function   : Blame the victim.
   Accepted by   : 47% or 146 participants

- Although most women wouldn't admit it, they generally like being physically forced to have sex.

   Thinking   : She wanted it.
   Function   : Trivialize the event:
   Accepted by   : 44% or 135 participants

- Most rape and sexual assaults are committed by strangers.

   Thinking : It is a deviant event; it rarely happens
   Function   : Trivialize the event
   Accepted by   : 44% or 137 participants

- Rape is unlikely to happen in a woman's own neighborhood.

   Thinking : It is a deviant event; it rarely happens
   Function   : Trivialize the event
   Accepted by   : 34% or 106 participants

- Many women secretly desire to be raped. She wanted It Trivialize the event. 98 (32%)

Thinking	: She wanted it
Function	: Trivialize the event
Accepted by	: 32 % 98 participants

- Usually, only women who wear sexy clothes are raped.

Thinking	: She asked for it
Function	: Blame the victim
Accepted by	: 26% or 81 participants

- If the rapist doesn't have a weapon, you really can't call it rape.

Thinking	: It wasn't really rape
Function	: Trivialize the event
Accepted by	: 18% or 54 participants

Points of Note

- Males accepted more rape myths than females.

- In a sample where 74 percent of the respondents were female, myths that excused the perpetrator and blamed the victim received the highest level of acceptance.

- It was noted that 75 percent of the group (n = 232) supported the idea that perpetrators do not usually intend to force sex on women, but sometimes became too aroused to control themselves. In a test-retest format, this statement received support a second time by 72 percent of the respondents (n = 227) indicating that this sentiment was strongly supported by the group.

- Seventy-six percent of the respondents (n = 234) accepted the statement that women should expect sex to be forced on them if they dressed in skimpy clothes, suggesting that perpetrators are not responsible for their own behavior, that is to say the women made them do it.

- Further, 72 percent (n = 221) believed that women generally lie about sexual violence, that they led men on, and then later claimed rape or assault as an act of revenge.

These results suggested that twelve years of educational experiences have been ineffective in making significant impact on rape-myth acceptance.

Question: What levels of healthy-relationship-myth acceptance existed among the selected graduating students?

Healthy-Relationship-Myth Acceptance: What Did the Results Show?

Individual Responses

Table 1: Healthy-Relationship-Myths Acceptance Levels

Stimulus: A healthy relationship is one in which your boyfriend or girlfriend loves you so much:

	Myth n – 311:	Theme	Acceptance Level
1.	They will do "anything" to please you.	Diffused psychological boundaries: expectation of no limitations or boundaries to their personal requests	242 (78%)
2.	You become totally committed to making them happy.	Assume responsibility for the other person's feelings	244 (78%)
3.	They get extremely jealous when you talk to someone else.	Control of the relationships	145 (47%)
4.	They always feel the need to be touching you.	Diffused physical boundaries: expected violation of personal space	134 (43%)
5.	They need to be with you during all of your free time.	Control your time	116 (37%)

Note: Healthy-relationship myths were considered accepted if endorsed by more than 37 percent of the respondents.

The assessment scale did not have as many healthy-relationship myths as it did rape myths. Of the 311 respondents, 245 participants, or 79 percent, were classified as high healthy-relationship-myth acceptors. Persons in this group accepted three to five of the five myths. Twenty one percent of their responses fell into the low-healthy-relationship-myth-acceptor group. Low acceptors accepted zero or one of the five myths.

Support was shown for collapsing all of one's personal boundaries and giving almost full control of one's life to the other partner once a relationship began. The study did not refer to marriage where the clause of being "one flesh" could be evoked. It specifically mentioned boyfriend or girlfriend relationships. Seventy-five percent of the respondents ($n = 244$) accepted that being in a boyfriend-girlfriend relationship "required" assuming responsibility for the other person's feelings. Seventy-eight percent of the participants ($n = 242$) accepted that being in a (boyfriend or girlfriend) relationship also meant that the partner should be willing to do "anything" the other partner requested. It was assumed that this "anything" would include allowing sexual contact even if it was not desired.

Question: What levels of response efficacy existed among the selected graduating students?

Response Efficacy: Constructive Responses in the Face of Victimization

Response efficacy as a general definition is the individual's perception or thinking that they can competently deliver a specified behavioral response. The delivered response should be able to make a positive difference in resolving an issue at hand. [9] There are two elements of response efficacy. First there is the *perception* that the capability to execute the behavior exists, and secondly, there is the *belief* that this behavior has the capacity to bring about the desired resolution to the presenting situation. Applied to the context of sexual violence, cognitions or thoughts of efficacy will influence the way individuals respond when faced with the opportunity to prevent an act of sexual violence. This is called the bystander response.

The bystander response as it relates to sexual-violence response efficacy suggests that an individual upon seeing a person in a risky situation in a social setting will respond to assist. The person will respond in the belief that he or she has the ability to prevent an act of sexual violence from occurring. The theory of constructive bystander responses suggests that the power of culturally embedded norms can be used to impact incidents of sexual violence. The thought is that in the same vein that tolerance of sexual violence can become normative; zero tolerance of sexual violence can also become a norm. Zero tolerance emerges if persons decide to intervene when they see an act of sexual violence occurring.

Impacting sexual-violence response efficacy can have an effect on incidents of sexual violence. This is so because enhancing response efficacy affects the individual's capacity to respond to prevent acts of sexual violence. It also influences the individual's ability to seek help when faced with victimization. For those who have already been victimized effective responding can prevent re-victimization. Persons are not likely to respond if there is diffusion of responsibility, [23] evaluation apprehension [59], or if perceived efficacy is low (i.e., there is the perceived absence of the personal capacity to intervene effectively).

High efficacy does not mean having to respond first. Even if persons decide to not be the first responders, they can decide to help the others who are trying to prevent the occurrence of an act of sexual violence. An example of this would be responding when seeing a young lady with behaviors symptomatic of intoxication being led away from a party by someone she does not know. This could also include seeing under-aged adolescents being sexually exploited and deciding to not ignore it.

Being able to respond effectively in these situations may significantly prevent acts of sexual violence.[19] McMahon and Baker (2011) noted:

> most assaults are committed by someone known to the victim, often involve alcohol intoxication and occur in social settings with others present...in these settings, bystanders are often present during the "preassault phase" where risk markers appear, and if equipped with the correct skills, can intervene to interrupt these situations. Hence, bystander intervention may be a potentially powerful prevention tool to ultimately reduce the occurrence of rape. In addition to primary prevention, bystanders can also respond after an assault occurs, providing support and resources to victims (p. 3)

Cognitions or thoughts of efficacy also influence the execution of help-seeking behaviors after being victimized. Post-victimization responses can mitigate the post-traumatic-stress responses associated with sexual violence. When post-traumatic stress is minimized, victims reduce the negative impact of the assault on their lives. Constructive post-victimization responses would involve seeking quality emotional care and attention that helps restore emotional balance, even if other legal and medical help is not pursued. In terms of post-victimization responses, most women go first to Health Services, followed by the police when there is violent physical assault. Other constructive responses include talking to a friend or family member, or contacting a crisis hotline. Most victims of sexual assault, adolescents included, do not seek help. [1,7,69] Young victims who chose to tell someone were likely to tell their mothers first. They also disclosed first to other family members but not as often to mothers. Within the Latin American and Caribbean region, only a small number of victims, regionally about 5 percent, disclose sexual violence. Ninety-five (95%) choose to remain silent.

Elements of Sexual-Violence Response Efficacy: Reasons for Silence

Sexual violence in Latin America and the Caribbean: A Desk Review (2010) noted the following reasons that many acts of violence are unreported:

Stigma, Shame

"I am damaged beyond repair," "I am ruined for life." In some communities, victims of sexual violence are considered "damaged" and are treated differently and not considered a premium choice for a partner. If they are in committed relationships, they fear being rejected by their partners.

Fear

Victims fear that the perpetrator will punish them for reporting the crime. If the violation occurred at the hands of an intimate partner, it is likely to happen again after being reported. There is fear, too, that other family members may be hurt by the angered perpetrator. If the perpetrator is part of the armed forces, is well known, and socially connected, there is greater fear of retaliation.

Overcomplicated Reporting Process

Too many steps are involved, the story has to be related too many times, too many other people's lives will be destroyed, and there will be too much hurting for too long with no perceived tangible results.

Guilt

Victims blame themselves or accept rape myths that blame them for the violation. Many persons accuse the victim of not struggling or resisting with enough force to deter the attacker—they did not do enough. Confidentiality structures were inadequate.

Lack of support

"No one is going to believe me, especially if the perpetrator is an acquaintance and people have seen us together." In some cases, the girls were punished by adults for "letting" someone rape them. Many persons discourage victims from reporting the incident. For many family members, the same perception that silences the victim, silences the families.

Post victimization responses that contribute to unveiling the identity of the perpetrator can contribute to reducing the incidence of sexual violence. Perpetrator behaviors that are not rewarded are eventually extinguished as perpetrators rely and thrive on secrecy, and silence. The extent that response efficacy can minimize secrecy is the extent to which a greater impact can be made on reducing incidents of sexual violence. Predators relying on secrecy are referred to as undetected predators. In the study of undetected sexual violators, it was noted that 120 of 1,882 incarcerated men recruited for the study admitted to committing about six undetected rapes each.[62] While 120 out of 1,882 may be a small percentage, this shows that this small percentage committed sexual violence against 720 persons. Many families were impacted and these acts were never punished. The variables that successfully silence victims directly enable the perpetrators.

Sexual Violence Response Efficacy: What Did The Results Show?

Individual Response

Table 2 Response Efficacy: Constructive Self-Help

Response	Likely n = 313	Not Sure	Unlikely
Tell a friend	191 (61%)	65 (21%)	55 (18%)
Tell parents	192 (62%)	66 (21%)	61 (17%)
Go to a hospital	172 (55%)	78 (25%)	61 (20%)
Go to the police	194 (62%)	63 (20%)	54 (17%)
Call a hotline	133 (43%)	97 (31%)	81 (26%)
Do nothing	52 (17%)	70 (23%)	189 (61%)

Note: The responses were based on the following stem: "If you were sexually violated by a male friend how likely is it that you would......" Participants were asked to express the likelihood of responding if violated. The perpetrator was hypothesized to be a male for both male and female respondents.

Three hundred and thirteen of the 314 questionnaires were used to assess response efficacy. Of the 313 respondents, 61 percent ($n = 189$) indicated that it was unlikely that they would do nothing if personally victimized. Table 5 shows that confiding in friends, calling the police, and telling parents were considered as likely options for self-help.

In terms of individual responses, 50 percent ($n = 155$) of the participants were placed in the high-response-efficacy category. These participants showed a high likelihood of seeking help for themselves as well as offering assistance to prevent a possible assault.

Table 3

Response Efficacy: Constructive Help for Others

	Response	Percentage
1.	Stay with her or find a trusted friend to be with her and make sure she is safe.	79 (25%)
2.	Do nothing. It is none of my business.	66 (21%)
3.	Ask her if she needs help.	147 (47%)
4.	Talk to the guy and ask where he is taking her.	21 (6%)

Note: The responses to this item were based on the following prompt: "You are at a party and you see a girl drinking and she appears to be very drunk. You see a man come and begin to lead her away from the party. Which of these would you do?"

Response Efficacy and the Impact of Socialization

It had been hypothesized that there would be low levels of response efficacy. This hypothesis was made given the empirical and theoretical premise that persons with high myth acceptance tend to blame and shame victims for their victimization. Since victims are perceived as being responsible for their own predicament, it was hypothesized that there would be less motivation for others to offer them assistance when they were in trouble. In addition to not being predisposed to helping others, high acceptors tend to also blame and shame themselves when victimized.

My study showed that despite the high level of myth acceptance, response-efficiency levels were not extremely low. Fifty percent of the respondents fell in the below average response-efficacy category and 50 percent fell in the above-average range. Though no group demonstrated very high levels of response efficacy, the scores were generally higher than expected given the high level of myth acceptance. Responses to questions assessing efficacy showed that despite their cognitions about sexual violence, 61 percent of the participants indicated that it would be unlikely that they would do nothing if victimized.

As a way of explanation, the challenge here may be one of perception. Sixty one percent (61%) of the participants indicated that it would be unlikely that they would do nothing if faced with offering assistance to a victim of potential sexual violence. These participants could have been thinking of sexual violence only in terms of bloody, near-death, violent attacks by strangers. In situations like these, they would not be too challenged to respond. The reality is that half of those who said they would do something in fact did nothing when tested.

They were given a story to demonstrate their possible response to victimization. Posttest questioning with some of the respondents showed that in some situations of acquaintance violations, statutory violations, sexual harassment, sexual assault, and other violations not involving near death, they would not act as competently as they predicted in the questionnaire. To a large extent, this supported the point that there is a misunderstanding of the qualitative experience of violence in sexual offences. It reinforced the notion that there is a need to help persons understand the multifaceted nature of sexual violence. The absence of blood does not mean the absence of violence. It stressed the continuing importance of having persons become aware of the existence of myths and to understand how mythology influences their response efficiency in situations of intimate partner violence, sexual assault, sexual harassment, and non-contact assault such as exhibitionism. A heightened level of awareness should raise the level of empowerment and response efficacy.

In summary then, a careful scrutiny was undertaken of the mythology of sexual violence, healthy-relationships and decision-making about how to efficiently respond in the face of victimization. Responses showed the impact of the infusion of the Jezebel-Madonna- Marianismo dilemma. This dilemma is characterized by conflict between the ideals of a conniving, sexually promiscuous, lustful, and immoral woman who can hardly be violated sexually (Jezebel) versus the ideal of a chaste, submissive, self-sacrificing, genteel lady (Madonna-Marianismo). Both of these interact with the ideal of the hypersexual, aggressive young male.

It was noted that responses to sexual victimization could be influenced by the extent to which the victim resembled the cultural Jezebel or Madonna. "She was not dressed decently that is why she was violated," "She was not supposed to be there so it is her fault," and "If she wanted to fraternize with men, that is what she got." If she looks like Jezebel, it wasn't really rape. If she blames the perpetrator, she should not be believed because Jezebels are lying and conniving. Exploration showed that these dynamics continued to shape students' ideals about femininity and masculinity and the prescribed relationships between the sexes.

What was validated was the need for a more effective curriculum-based intervention that could make a more indelible impact on students' cognitions associated with sexual violence. Curriculum interventions are needed to confront the mythology, uproot the stereotypes and show perpetrators to be responsible for their actions. Someone is violated because

<u>someone</u> <u>chose</u> to violate them. There were some elements that spurred a sense of hope:

- There was a failure to accept the myth that only women in skimpy clothes were violated.
- It was also good to note that myths that trivialized sexual violence were rejected.

Note: Students from private schools were not included in the study because they were not exposed to the national risk reduction curriculum implementation project that formed the basis for the study. Further, based on the sampling technique used, the majority of the participants ended up being students who resided in what could be called high risk communities. Seventy-five percent of the participants were female. This was a relatively accurate reflection of the graduation ratio of males to females at the upper secondary level during that time period.

Acceptance of myths and cultural messages in and of themselves do not increase the predisposition to become sexually violent. Acceptance of rape myths and the associated messages coupled with a predisposition to engage in aggressive behavior increases the likelihood of committing an act of sexual violence.

Up to this point discussion has centered on the high levels of myth acceptance. The reality of response efficacy has also been analyzed. The next chapter discusses ways that parents and teachers can reduce support for sexual violence.

5

ENHANCING TEACHER AND PARENTING CAPACITY TO REDUCE SEXUAL VIOLENCE

t is important to begin this section with a statement of empowerment. One person "can" make a significant difference in the way we understand and respond to sexual violence. This is important to remember because there will be times when you may find yourself standing alone defending some issues against majority perceptions and opinions.

- **Educate Yourself** to be able to challenge sexual-violence fatigue. Persons around you may be sick and tired of hearing about sexual violence. They may believe that they have heard all there is to hear. To avoid falling into that mind-set, make it a point to continually clarify the assumptions you make about sexuality and violence. Make an effort to increase your comfort with discussing the topic. Continually assess your own knowledge, attitude, and perceptions about sexualization and victimization. This will help you to be able to recognize and respond to wrong thinking and behavior when you hear and see it. Part of that education should involve becoming more familiar with the legal definition of sexual violence including noncontact sexual violence (threatened sexual violence, exhibitionism, verbal sexual harassment, exposure to pornography). Completed and attempted sexual violence are both criminal.

- **Expand the Limits**. Understand all of the different aspects of consent, that is, those unable to consent because of age, mental challenges including IQ, and psychological manipulation (trickery, deceit). It is important to stress that the absence of bloodshed is not a viable definition of consent. Forcing your will on somebody by trickery, deceit, and or psychological pressure is also violence.

- **Eliminate the Confusion**. Emphasize that all behavior is a matter of choice. An individual is violated because someone "chooses" to violate them regardless of any other factor involved in the situation. It is important to not blame the victim for the behavior of the perpetrator.

- **Remove the Veil**. Sexual violence is not only about the stranger in the dark with a knife or gun. Give attention to the fact that sexual violence can happen in homes, on the streets, at school. It usually takes place on a continuum, beginning with grooming. Grooming is the process used by perpetrators to slowly allow victims to become comfortable with their offending behavior. The grooming process allows targeted victims to become comfortable with the persons who will eventually violate them. A properly groomed victim is less likely to report the offense. Recognize that males can be victims too. See table 4 below.

- **Listen to Yourself**. While disciplining or teaching, ensure that your communication does not support irresponsible sexual behavior in the way you talk about the construction of the masculine identity. This becomes a real danger when discussing characteristics of "real" men. An example of this would be directly telling or having persons understand and believe that sexual and violent behaviors are beyond a "real" man's control. Another problematic response would be to suggest that behaviors indicative of self-control are somehow effeminate or 'soft'.

- **Listen Again to Yourself.** Ensure that what you say does not reaffirm irresponsible subservience in the construction of the feminine identity. These statements usually talk about what a woman is "supposed to" or "must" tolerate if she is to be viewed as a "good woman." What is said in this context should not reaffirm the cultural commoditization or transactional nature of relationships where focus is placed on any material benefits that may be derived from supporting or tolerating sexual violation.

- **Screen Your Emotions**. The emotional tone of instructional language is critically important. Listen carefully to yourself when you are teaching or talking to children about concepts related to sexual violence themes. Is your language positive? Is it inclusive? Is it empowering? Is it gender specific? Does it make reference to gender-based issues in a clear manner, free of derogatory, or slang expressions? Be especially careful about how you define and use common words like "hoe" (whore), slut, sissy, soft, dog (reference to unacceptable male behavior),'wutless' (worthless).
- **Victimization is not Death**. Be careful not to equate sexual violation with annihilation, a disaster from which a victim can never recover. Such expressions give more power to the perpetrator. Someone who has been victimized is not automatically ruined for life.

Table 4

Grooming Techniques of Predators

Grooming Techniques for Younger Targets	Grooming Techniques for Older Targets
1. Makes efforts to systematically decrease space between self and targeted person 2. Plays body contact games (lifting off the ground games, hugging and holding tight games, tickling, backrubs, wrestling) 3. Gradually moves physical contact into the intimate and personal range 4. Pretends to accidentally enter the private space when the targeted child is undressing 5. Takes advantage of the child's natural curiosities about sexuality 6. Encourages 'harmless' secrets in preparation for later sexual secrets	• Presents a social façade of being a couple ensuring that significant others see them together in a very public way to prepare for a defense in case an accusation is made after the fact • Gets to know the likes and dislike of the target paying them special focused attention, buying them gifts • Gradually isolates target with increasing frequency (taking them on special outings where they can be alone) • Takes advantage of natural curiosities about sexuality • Desensitizes youth by introducing sexualized topics to test boundaries • Shows pictures or pornographic images to normalize the behavior. • Encourages 'harmless' secrets in preparation for later sexual secrets gradually making physical contact more intimate and personal without seeking consenting responses

Note: This information was adapted from REACH. University of Minnesota https://reachmilitaryfamilies.umn.edu/sites/default/files/rdoc/ Safeguarding%20

Pay Attention to your Message. Ensure that your messages do not blame the victim, make excuses for the perpetrator, re-victimize the victim, and promote gender discrimination. Here are some messages that could inadvertently be transmitted:

(a) The victim asked for it (sexual violence).
(b) Don't pay attention to the victim because the victim does not really know what sexual violence means.
(c) Victims misunderstand the "perpetrator's intention" because he "could not have meant" the behaviour to be rape/sexual violence.
(d) The victim misunderstood her "own intentions." She was not sure of what she saying, doing, wanted.
(e) The victim is always a liar, if not criminal at least she/he is unethical. Don't trust what she says
(f) The victim is exaggerating the impact that the violation has had.
(g) Sexual violence is not a normative event; there is a big chance that no violence occurred because sexual violence is a rare phenomenon.

- **Beware of Short Cuts**. There are times in discussions, complex questions about violence and consent may arise. There may be the urge to spontaneously advise children to "wait until you are sixteen" as a panacea for many of these complex issues that arise. When talking about consent and the age of consent, be careful not to present sixteen as the magical age that promises legal authority for high-risk, unethical sexual behavior. A more effective response would involve creating interactive discussions and activities that (a) show how to cope with peer pressure for premature sexual activity, (b) teach how to analyze the forces in the environment that support sexual violence, (c) demonstrate effective problem-solving skills, and (d) provide referral for professional peer or adult counseling for more detailed responses on sexual and reproductive health and rights issues. Attaining the legal age of consent does not equate to being intellectually, spiritually, or emotionally ready to consent or to negotiate the process of consent.

- **Encourage Critical Thinking**. Questions and activities should help children explore the ways that they may have been socialized to violate consent or to accept the violation of consent. Help children to challenge rape myths and victim blaming. Help them learn the characteristics of situations that present great risk for violation.

- **Empowerment is Important**. Emphasize the importance of clear, assertive communication at all times. Have persons remember that drugs and alcohol are sometimes used as weapons to lessen their ability to make decisions that will protect them. Drunk or inebriated persons who are not in full control of their behavior are more likely to become either victims or perpetrators of sexual violence than a sober person. So being with someone intoxicated can place a person at an increased risk of being assaulted.

- **Zero Tolerance is Critical**. Provide information about effective responses to victimization as a bystander. When friends unite and decide that they will not remain silent or motionless in the face of potential or known victimization, the incidents of sexual violence should decrease. Perpetrators need to expect consequences. Provide information about where to go for help even if only to talk

Even if the victim chooses not to pursue a legal response, the perpetrator will still know that their prey was not rendered powerless by fear. This may act as a deterrent to some small degree.

What Schools Can Do: Curriculum Implementation Evaluation

The Health and Family Life Education (HFLE) curriculum is the direct mechanism for the Government influencing sexual-violence risk reduction in the Bahamian community. The recommendations made below are cost-effective responses that would enhance the capacity of a national

HFLE curriculum to make a more significant impact on cognitive correlates of sexual violence. The objective of the recommendations is to improve efforts to maximize already-existing resources. This approach is taken knowing that in many situations, resources are limited and teachers already have challenges responding to the demands of their schedules. Any recommendations that would involve more work, more money, and more time requirements are likely to be met with resistance and abandonment.

My study showed that despite our best efforts, there is a need to enhance the schools' potential to impact cognitions associated with sexual violence. Evaluation is needed. Sample curriculum implementation evaluation questions could include:

- To what extent has curriculum-based information on sexual-violence prevention been presented in a format that has reinforced the idea that women invite or cause sexual violence? Sometimes the discussion of self-protection strategies may leave the impression that there are some things that women could do to *prevent* sexual violence and protect themselves, but the act of violence is always the responsibility of the aggressor. So *risk reduction* rather than prevention should be the focus when addressing girls. Prevention becomes the focus when addressing boys. However, given the reality that both males and females can be predators, careful language considerations are important based on the context of discussions.
- To what extent have curriculum-based sexual-violence-prevention techniques focused only on stranger-perpetrated violence?
- To what extent have curriculum-based sexual-violence-prevention techniques enhanced participants' awareness of the way that their gender identities and relationship expectations are being influenced by the media, family, peer pressure, and their own needs? To what extent has the curriculum given them the skills to challenge these realities?

- To what extent have curriculum-based sexual-violence-prevention techniques been limited to a one-time, thirty-minute didactic presentation by an invited speaker who makes an emotional appeal and then leaves?
- To what extent do curriculum-based sexual-violence-prevention techniques use culturally sensitive local data, statistics, and experiences in presentations?
- To what extent do curriculum-based sexual-violence-prevention techniques highlight the power of bystander intervention and provide the skills to subtly or assertively intervene in a safe manner?
- To what extent do curriculum-based sexual-violence-prevention techniques enable small-scale gender-homogenous group discussions, co-ed presenters, or presenter representation of other ethnic-immigrant groups that live in the school's communities?
- To what extent do curriculum-based sexual-violence-prevention techniques integrate concepts of human rights, bullying, and healthy relationships so that the concept of sexual violence is not discussed in isolation?

A Systems Approach

Senior curriculum officers with responsibility for Health and Family Education can form a working committee to focus on conducting short-term sexual violence risk reduction curriculum evaluation exercises. This committee could be made up of representatives of HFLE teachers, guidance counselors, and other stakeholders. The goal of the committee would be to review the risk-reduction curricula practices, and assess the extent that these practices match guidelines for best practices in the field of risk-reduction education with a specific reference to sexual violence. On the basis of the review, a teacher friendly "best practice" booklet can be produced as a resource that will enhance curriculum-implementation fidelity. This pamphlet should especially be geared toward teachers uncomfortable with the content area/topic of sexual violence.

Use existing human and curriculum resources to assist in initiating a short-term district or national drive toward sexual-violence risk reduction. In the Bahamas, the existing resources would be those created by the -Focus-on-Youth-Caribbean implementation program. The FOY-C curriculum-implementation team over the years has trained hundreds of teachers, parents, and some principals in the interactive pedagogical and parenting skills. These skills are known to be effective for impacting cognitions. The Bahamas' Ministry of Education, HFLE-FOY- C senior education office maintains a list of these teachers and parents along with their addresses and phone contact information. A group of competent teachers and parents can be recruited and have their training upgraded to equip them to function as a resource in a national initiative.

Parent Resource Groups. The parent group can offer assistance to members of parent-teacher associations, church-parent groups, and other community entities in implementing short-term regional initiatives. They can contribute expertise on the impact that parenting and cultural norms have on supporting cognitions that facilitate sexual violence. They can provide input on parenting techniques for sexual-violence risk reduction.

HFLE Teacher-advocacy Group. The primary objective of this group would be to use peer influence in raising the level of priority given by their colleagues to the HFLE segment of the curriculum. A teacher-training support group can also offer moral and technical support in helping teachers give more attention to effective pedagogy for this content area. This should function to increase the desire to complete curriculum requirements for HFLE when faced with inevitable scheduling conflicts. This group can encourage their peers to regularly do personal assessments to evaluate the extent that their own knowledge, attitudes, beliefs, and perceptions are compatible with norms that do not support sexual violence or other forms of high-risk behavior.

Add Administrative Value to the Content: Make It Examinable

School administrators can establish minimum graduation requirements that include the completion of a series of personal-development work-shops (transition-to-graduation workshops).

- Excerpts from risk-reduction curricula can be used to formulate learning objectives and establish criteria for successful comple-tion. "Transition-to-graduation" seminars can be held throughout grades ten and eleven to facilitate student exposure to a series of life-skill workshops. These workshops should address not just the factual narratives but create opportunities to evoke cognitive dis-sonance for beliefs supportive of sexual violence. The workshops can address cognitive correlates of dysfunctional behavior that im-pacts all areas of functioning—sexual violence just being one of them.

Some schools exempt their more academically competent students from life-skills content classes because the HFLE content is devalued. However, more academically competent students were included in this study and to a limited extent the results reflect some of their opinions as well. Students can be given a small but important baseline assessment or pretest on life-skills issues and have a posttest done at the end of grade twelve when they would have completed the planned series. Making life-skills development examinable highlights its value in the eyes of students and staff.

Administrative Support for Integration. The reality is that many schools may not have the resources to timetable HFLE. Also, there are teachers who may be uncomfortable with the topic and hope for some-one else to cover the content area. Without administrative oversight, both groups of teachers are vulnerable to neglecting the content area. This is especially so if they perceive administrative support for this neg-ligence. The study showed that when teachers were left to integrate the content area wherever they found a teachable moment, less impact on cognitions was noted. These were the children in the undefined group.

Hence, even if resources, values, and interests do not permit a separate subject area for HFLE, administrative supervision and training and support are necessary to help them support teachers in their efforts to integrate the content. This should minimize the urge of all to abandon the important issues of HFLE in the face of timetable pressure or personal discomfort. There are many related themes within the topic of sexual-violence risk reduction that can be integrated throughout the curriculum, , including assertive communication, gender roles, cultural-force-field analysis, gender-identity construction, relationship-development strategies, and human and civil rights. Many risk-reduction curricula offer an array of integrated, sequential themes that help teachers present the topic from a broad perspective. Many curriculum guidelines instruct the teacher almost word for word on how to facilitate classes. If Administrators become aware of this, they can better assist the integration efforts.

Begin early. Formally and in small doses begin integrating early discussion of violence, human rights, self-empowerment, and body rights at the primary-school level. This will set the foundation for the more mature content series of curriculum at the high-school level. Talking about good and bad touches is a good beginning but it is not enough.

6

OTHER CHILDREN'S STORIES

These excerpts from my book *african children* cry show the complexity of some aspects of the social cultural milieu that dislocates our children and exacerbate the impact of sexual violence

Part 1: Complicated Peer Issues

1. **Mudda Sick** (narrative of a student father, a true story)

My gal 13 and pregnant, mudda sick NOW! Dey tell me use condom but didn't say HOW!
Don't need to worry, from dis I ga walk, I too young for dem to take me to court.
I should play fool, say baby ain't mine, I only been dere dat one time, mudda sick Boo
What D-i suppose to do, my head screw! I too young and dis ain't right, but I ain't
        ga let her pregnancy jam up my life.

My ole lady wan know what I tellin her for, she ain't gat nuff for us, much less one more, Don't wan nobody parents crowdin her door, I hate to see her pregnant, sad, out of school, I like her, it ain't fair, and it ain't cool! She wan me come over to visit and talk, I hail, chat fast, and speed walk, I gat exam; for a girl her age, she gat homicide rage.
   Mudda sick, no money and baby due; we fix dis pot but can't
        eat the stew.

I bring my Saturday $50 tip and tip in awe, glad for the time to play with son on the floor
She yuck my son from my hand, for her new man, take my fiddy dollars and run me off dey land.
Passin' the gate, anger heavy in my hand, my son and my girl playin with another man,
Mudda sick dread I can't pay, can't play, ain't gat nuttin to say, gat to hurry forward in school,

Advantaged by that single parent, 'no-daddy' rule.

2. SOFT BOY (a student's narrative of male exploitation)

Dese gals round here don't wan be wid me; say I is a *SOFT BOY*, I don't have no SUV
My plain *SOFT BOY* shirt ain't enough ya see, say I must wear Johns, Figgers or fresh Tommy!
Give me dollar, give me snack, give me phone card, or get tax, geemee dis, and geemee dat!
Don't get it; dey trippin; and me and dem sittin in <u>same</u> student position, yet I must find money, to pay.
For SOFT BOY extortion, they say

Geemee gals organize, ya'll; beggin, shamin, always on call; without work, 100 dollars a night, money from fellas scared of gals who ga call dem 'light'; fellas too afraid to say 'no,' always ready for a show; Geemee gals gat dem all in tow; Not studyin, I start work, packin grocery till it hurt; when Geemee gals beg me, I free of the shame of having 'Broke Nigga' added to my name, I now a Geemee gals'
man, with extra money in my hand

G.P.A. down below 3.3; extortion stoppin' now ya see! when next Geemee gals beg,
I claimin' my 'SOFT BOY'; I ain't scared; I say this for me, "Dis soft boy here, he gone free,
don't mistake me no more fa ya sad, missin' daddy"; You turn around and complain,
How black man, dey always broke, but we lock in ya geemee, geemee choke.
But this soft boy makin a change,

I takin a stand; givin you my money doesn't make me man; I step-pin' off your geemee plan;
hey I is a real man; against all User' scheme and plan, I straight, not lookin' fa fame
I too smart to play dat game; call me SOFT, I ain't shame; a 'SOFT BOY' is a sensible man.
he usin' he head to tink and plan; So call me SOFT, call me hater, I ga have money now
And I ga have money later!

3. **Udda Niggas' Gun**

(victim narrative of a gang fight, the ending fictionalized to emphasize a point)

Udder Nigga grip my shirt man; slam me hard on my thigh
I whap him wid my cutlass, I burst 2 bottle in he eye.
Dey throw more rock on me, one burst me on my chin.
My boys run dem down and cave dey bloody head in
Four dey boys try rush us, thought they was slick for sure;
swing round wid da big knife and slice up four more;
Don't' think this finish yet; yo, homey I get my gun!
If you want live, Udder Nigga, you'll better start ya run

Down the road *first* walking, *now* runnin, runnin for my life.
Knife and cutlass, can't help me now, dis a all out death fight.
Could hear the gunshot comin as Udder Niggas drive past.
Could hear the siren screamin, blood pumpin, bleedin fast.
Darkness comin from every, where, none a my boys in sight.
Face down in the loneliness, Jah know erryting aight.
I glad my gal was watchin, watchin how suicidal I fight,
for sure she *now* know I een like Udder Niggas, I een light;

Before my gal talk to Udder Niggas again, I know she ga tink twice,
She better come see me, I dress to kill, coffin white, chillin wid my
boys still
Scripture, solos, eulogy aight; wait, how come nobody braggin
bout how good I could a fight; why Mamma won't stop screaming,
sisters and brothers ill on the floor; hey you'll, big me up some
more!
Yo where my gal is, my gal needs to come tell you'll the tale,
how I cause Udder Niggas dem get lost in jail, get my legacy right,
I wasn't light, 'talkin to my gal', that was the cause of this death
fight!"

Part 2: Complicated Family Issues

1. **Poison Conch Salad** (a child's perception of her father's 'outside' children)

One full sister, and one full brother, of my daddy and my mother, live with my daddy-mother, on the eastern side of Johnson Rd, and the one half -brother, from my lovely mother, live with he daddy, near the old red church in the Grove.

I sorry for my oldest half -sister, also from my mother, who lived with the girlfriend of mother's half- brother, until they fell out and she had to move back in wid her ex -fella, cause girlfriend of mother half -brother, throw sister's new man out.

Now my youngest half-sister daddy, he does work to the chicken shack, when he bring food for my sister, it is be enough to eat and pack but mother new jealous boyfriend Claude, say he stoppin dat, no bringin food for he new family behind he back.

My mother new boyfriend old girl friend other children's daddy, does give his children lunch, but if my mother new boyfriend old girlfriend, wan feed the children she had wid him, she gata sell backwood, Tribune, Guardian and Punch

My 2 half- brothers, from my father, live in Fox Hill by the tree stump, I see them all the time on my way to the pump, now half -brothers of my father, dey go to private school, dey fees pay, but father, with my mother, always playin da fool.

Mother say next time father come here, look behind he ear, and I'll see where she mark him wid edge tool, but my father he een stupid, he dress up drivin mother of half-brother jeep, so busy takin my half-brother dem to school, mother can't ketch him nah, he way too cool.

But my mother say not to worry about a thing, father and half-brother mother won't go far, my father only with she, long as he could drive she new car, the first time he can't afford to put gas in her jeep, he'll be right back round here lookin for place to sleep.

Some families really mix up though, before you have children, there aint no doubt, you must call a family reunion to straighten your blood line out, I don't know what this conch salad about, and why can't parents put all dey chirren in the same family, in the same house?

2. **Mudda Girlfriend** (child's story of her mother's lesbianism)

Mudda girlfriend was waiting for me outside the shop, she tink I scared a she, she better stop, she say she hard, but me I born tough, she wan take over my family, she wan play rough.

I look round to see if anyone hear, dis big teeth red woman, with her beer, and orange hair, trying to cause me fear, I look round, pick up one rock, I fling it and just miss the shop.

She say, girl I don't understand your problem wid me and ya ma, I take care a you'll better than ya'll no good pa, respect da love between me and ya ma, dis hate for me gone too far.

Don't be fool, talkin family business to school, if dey ask about we, we ga say no, we find you to be uncontrollable; make up ya mind what it ga be, respect for our love or fulltime war wid me.

You better get use to it girl, we is a couple, we done out, I tired a you troublin me when I come round dat house; sweet girl, I gat clout, get with the program or you could get out.

Out- to every man and boy I went, to get rid of da stench a da woman scent, my bruddas and sisters to foster care went, we all over the place until the police brought us back to our mudda place

My mudda leave dat girlfriend, she got a younger man; I try to stay home with step daddy friendly hand, I fightin, holding the tide, but mudda and girlfriend sneakin on the side.

3. **Crazy Nigga** (teenager's experience of mother's new boyfriend)

Dis Nigga playin bae, he better stop.
Dis house jam up and dis hard floor hot!
How long, he ga be here, holdin up my room?
Doon live here, and he een wan go home!

You een my daddy, son, in here, lazy leg cross!
Can't touch me Cappy, in here I is da boss!
Twice a day, 7 on da hour, dis stupid Nigga in here,
hoggin up our shower, bold; but *I* gat power!

In da kitchen here, openin pot on stove.
Dis nigga wan us get up, and iron *he* clothes!
My ma playin in he hair, she freakin on he knee,
Wan *my* sisters get up to make dis man tea

"Shet ***** up", he like to holler,
searchin my ma bag for condoms and dollar.
Callin he gals dem, loud my ma cell in he hand,
dis nigga say he ga teach *me* to be a man!!!

Steppin over my brudders, dem sleepin on da hard floor,
Tax dis nigga man, he doin for more! gata work this out,
change this plan *I* ga teach this nigga to be a man!
Cause me move out to live with my gal Ruby-Ann,

I start ta beat dis crazy man, slap him roun, break he teet,
He een no daddy over we, put a hold on him, he couldn't go far
"You'll leave him" mudda say, "I gats needs and bills to pay,
Don't want you'll gettin in my way, find ya sef some place to stay!"

4. **Drug Lady** (a young man's tale of maternal substance abuse and prostitution)

Heard my friends brag, bout one ole hag,
Exchanging best sex for little money.
Hopped in the car, they said it wasn't far.
I should see and be with this Honey.
Dollars in my shirt, a little fun won't hurt
and I ran in full haste for fun car.
Underage drivers speed, hurry to fill a need,
for some fun from this ole Honey.
As the car turned, the bend, the journey
came to an end as the old hag was my
cocaine-addicted, old lady.

4. **Abortion** (a true story)

My pretty ma tired beat me from round my boyfriend door; without shame, pretty me, go back, each day, afterschool for more; she say dat my man old enough to be her man, one day she may even try her hand; she say "stay from round dat man, stay out he car, stop drinkin' wid him in da corner bar, you only 13 girl is a sin to see, how you lettin' da man get ya tings for free, make sure he wrap it up, so you don't ketch disease; I don't want nuttin destroy my life of ease.'

The 14th of the month must be an important date, my man always checkin' to see if Red- water late; don't worry, you could be sure, on the 14, Red-water always came knockin' at the front door; da first time my man see Red-water run, he get scared, say free-stylin' done; he has to get a good protection plan; must show respect for dat Red-water man; Reds must come once a month ya see, so my boyfriend-man could stay jail- free, he could stay free to take care me.

I couldn't understand this weird thing you see, Red-water was more important than me; every second week of the four, boyfriend must check the front door; when one day Red-water was late, boyfriend gone crazy, starin' at the door; sayin' he "catchin' the horse before it leave the gate; he need to do that ting; to do it before it too late"; what horse, what gate, what ting, what late; someone need to explain this meal on my plate!

My boyfriend buy this funny stick-ting, made me water in cup, waitin for blue ring; blue ring came, everything change; slap me in my face say pretty gal ga cause him big disgrace; boyfriend crazy, he actin' strange; things he says must change, 800 dollars, phone card, doctor phone number I must carry these to my pretty mother; thought I did catch dat disease what mama did dread, I take dem tings and put dem under my bed, I sick, vomitin' and scarred, I ga dead.

My ma suddenly take notice, I was broke, not pretty and not cute, 'what happen gal why you look sick', I tell her bout the Red-water, cup and blue ring on the lil' stick; whap, one back hand slap, two licks wid one shoe, she broke up the fan while smashin' up dishes and flingin' da fryin' pan too; how come I never tell her I did not see the Red-water- man; you pregnant gal dats for sure, but no baby comin' through that young door, wid my hair in she hand, went to find my man.

When we get in front he house, she took her stand, with big stick in hand she started to shout, "Bring your black you know what out," one other lil' pretty neighbour girl come runnin' out he door; boyfriend come out smilin' half dressed in shame in front he door, what he was smiling bout I wasn't sure; my ma grip him, body slam him on he floor; I watch mother all through the fight, beat him bad, wonderin' why it took her so long to make things right.

It was strange to see, it look like she really did care bout me, when I look, she was holdin he pants waist and breathin' rum down he face, "I want money and I want it now, Sell dem gold teet, sell ya car," My brudda if you tink it funny, come back round here without dat money; no one explained nothing to me; I told ma bout da money I hide from she, the money he done did give me; not to worry I will see, they will get a doctor to take the disease-ring out my pee.

"Just do what the doctor say and da problem would go away; they hoped you see doctor bring, Red-water and pretty back to me; if red-water came back to me, things would return to how they use to be; just as planned, taken to doctor- man, and my red-water man came back to me; weeks later all is well, I hear the school bell, must hurry and not be late; yet somethin' in my mind just ain't fine as mother again tried to explain this thing to me:

"When ya Red-water came down, that mean I was wrong, bout there being a baby there ya see; the blue ring on the stick was a little trick, to see if you was disease free, the doctor did give you a Vitamin see, to stop Red-water turnin' to a real baby; mother had no fear, boyfriend was clear said I would be straight soon with money too; in school chair hair, it all became clear when Tru' Gossip sat close to my ear, say she hear, my abortion clear but don't fear, cuz she been there too.

References

1. Ahrens, C. E. 2006. "Being Silenced: The Impact of Negative Social Reactions on the Disclosure of Rape." *American Journal of Community Psychology* 38 (3—4): 263–d74. doi: 10.1007/s10464-006-9069-9.

2. "Adolescent Sexual Assault: Update of the Literature." *Growing Up Too Quickly: Children Who Lose Out on Their Childhoods*, edited by C. Bardin. *Paediatrics and Child Health* 10 (5): 264–69. Also available at http://www.ncbi.nlm.nih.gov/pmc/articles/PMC2722541/

3. AIDS Support and Technical Assistance Resources [AIDSTAR-One]. 2011. "Caribbean Regional HIV Prevention Summit on MARP Most-At-Risk Populations and OVP Other Vulnerable Populations. Available at http://www.aidstar-one.com/sites/default/files/AIDSTAR-http://www.aidstar-one.com/sites/default/files/AIDSTAR-one._MeetingReport_CaribbeanPrevSummit_Mar2011.pdf.

4. Amnesty International Secretariat. 2007. *Sexual Violence against Women and Girls in Jamaica: Just a Little Sex.* Available at http://www.bawp.org/Resources/Documents/jamaicafinal.pdf.

5. Anderson, L. A., and Whiston, S. C. 2005. "Sexual Assault Education Programs: A Meta-analytic Examination of Their Effectiveness." *Psychology of Women Quarterly* 29:: 374–88.

6. APA. (American Psychological Association) (2008). Task Force on Sexualization of Girls. Washington, DC http://www.apa.org/pi/women/programs/girls/report.aspx

7. Atkinson, M. A. 2008. "A Parent's Guide to Helping a Daughter Who Has Been Raped." Available at http://www.resurrectionafterrape.org/media/Rape%20-parents%20guide.pdf.

8. Baldwin, A. L. 1980. *Theories of Child Development*. New York: John Wiley & Sons.

9. Banyard, V. L., and Moynihan, M. M. 2011. "Variation in Bystander Behavior Related to Sexual and IPVP Intimate Partner Violence Prevention: Correlates in a Sample of College Students." *Psychology of Violence* 1 (4): 287—301. doi: 10.1037/a0023544.

10. Berkowitz, A. 2010. "Fostering Healthy Norms to Prevent Violence." In *The Prevention of Sexual Violence: A Practitioner's Sourcebook*, edited by K. Kaufman. NEARI Press. Also available at http://www.alanberkowitz.com/articles/Preventing%20Sexual%20Violence%20Chapter%20-%20Revision.pdf.

11. Blank, L. 2005. *The Situation of Youth in the Bahamas*. Prepared for the Government of the Bahamas & the Inter-American Development Bank. Ministry of Youth: Nassau, Bahamas.

12. Bohner, G., Jarvis, C. L., Esyssel, F., and Siebler, F. 2005. "The Causal Impact of Rape Myth Acceptance on Men's Rape Proclivity: Comparing Sexually Coercive and Noncoercive Men." *European Journal of Social Psychology* 35 (6): 819—28. doi: 10.1002/ejsp.284.

13. Borduin, C. M., Schaeffer, C. M., and Heiblum, N. 2009. "Randomized Clinical Trial of Multisystemic Therapy with Juvenile Sexual Offenders: Effects on Youth Social Ecology and Criminal Activity." *Journal of*

Consulting and Clinical Psychology 77 (1:): 26—37. doi: 10.1037/a0013035. Also available at http://psycnet.apa.org/journals/ccp/77/1/26.pdf.

14. Bouffard, L. A., and Bouffard, J. A. 2011. "Understanding Men's Perceptions of Risks and Rewards in a Date Rape Scenario." *International Journal of Offender Therapy and Comparative Criminology* 55 (4:): 626—45. doi: 10.1177/0306624X10365083.

15. Brownmiller, S. 1975. *Against Our Will.* Available at www.susanbrownmiller.com/susanbrownmiller//html/against_our_will.html.

16. Brownmiller, S. 2000 "Thornhill: Rape on the B." Brain." Review of *Natural History of Rape: Biological Bass of SC Sexual Coercion,* by R. Thornhill, and C. Palmer.www.susanbrownmiller.com/susanbrownmiller/html/review-thornhill.html.

17. Bryden, D. P., and Grier, M. M. 2011. "The Search for Rapists' 'Real Motives.' *Journal of Criminal Law & Criminology* 101 (1). : http://scholarlycommons.law.northwestern.edu/cgi/viewcontent.9&context=jclc.

18. Caceres, C. 2005. "Assessing Young People's Nonconsensual Sexual Experiences: Lessons from Peru." In *Sex Without Consent: Young People in Countries Developing Countries,* edited by S. J. Jejeebhoy, I. Shah and S. Thapa. London: Zed Books. Also available at http://www.iessdeh.org/usuario/ftp/SEXWITHOUT.pdf.

19. Casey, E. A. and Kristin Ohler. 2011. "Being a Positive Bystander: Male Antiviolence Allies' Experiences of 'Stepping Up.'" Abstract. *Journal of Interpersonal Violence* 27,1 62—83. doi: 10.1177/0886260511416479.

20. CDC.. 2015.. *Sexual Violence: Definitions.* http://www.cdc.gov/violenceprevention/sexualviolence/definitions.html.

21. CDC. 2016. *Sexual Violence: Consequences.* http://www.cdc.gov/violenceprevention/sexualviolence/definitions.html.

22. Chapleau, K. M., Oswald, D. L., and Russell, B. L. 2008. "Male Rape Myths: The Role of Gender, Violence, and Sexism." *Journal of Interpersonal Violence* 23 (5:): 600—15. doi:10.1177/0886260507313529.

23. Chekroun, P.and Brauer, M. 2002. "The Bystander Effect and Social Control Behavior: The Effect of the Presence of Others on People's Reactions to Norm Violations. *European Journal of Social Psychology* 32: 853–67. Also available at http://lapsco.univ-bpclermont.fr/persos/brauer/pdf/Chekroun%20%26%20Brauer,%202002,%20EJSP.pdf.

24. Chiroro, P., Bohner, G. G., Viki. T., and Jarvis, C. I. 2004. "Rape Myth Acceptance and Rape Proclivity: Expected Dominance versus Expected Arousal as Mediators in Acquaintance-Rape Situations. *Journal of Interpersonal Violence* 19:: 427—41. doi:10.1177/0886260503262081.

25. Cohn, E. S., Dupuis, E. C., and Brown, T. M. 2009. "In the Eye of the Beholder: Do Behavior and Character Affect Victim and Perpetrator Responsibility for Acquaintance Rape?" *Journal of Applied Social Psychology* 39 (7:): 1513—35. doi:10.1111/j.1559-1816.2009.00493.x.

26. Coker, A. L., Cook-Craig, P. G., Williams, C. M., Fisher, B. S., and Cleare, E. R. 2011. "Evaluation of Green Dot: An Active Bystander Intervention to Reduce Sexual Violence on College Campuses. *Violence Against Women* 20 (10:): 1—20. doi: 10.1177/1077801211410264.

27. Contreras, J. M. 2005. "Conflict within Intimacy: A Socio-Demographic Analysis of Male Involvement in IPV Intimate Partner Violence in Mexico." PhD diss.., London School of Medicine and Tropical Medicine. Available at http://researchonline.lshtm.ac.uk/682337/1/420865.pdf.

28. Contreras, J. M., Bott, S., Guedes, A., Danielson, C. K., and Holmes, M. M. 2004. DeGue, S., Massetti, G. M., Holt, M. K., Tharp, A. T., Valle, L. A., Matjasko, J. L., and Lippy, C. 2013. "Identifying Links between Sexual Violence and Youth Violence Perpetration: New Opportunities for Sexual Violence Prevention. *Psychology of Violence* 3 (2:): 140—56. doi:10.1037/a0029084.

29. Edmonds, W. A. and Kennedy, T. D. 2012. *An Applied Reference Guide to Research Design: Quantitative, Qualitative and Mixed Methods.* Thousand Oaks, CA: Sage.

30. Ellis, L. 1991. "A synthesized (Biosocial) Theory of Rape." *Journal of Consulting and Clinical Psychology* 59 (5:): 631—42.

31. Fawcett, B. (2013) Violence against women: current theory and practice in domestic abuse, sexual violence and exploitation. *Feminist Review* 2013,**112,** e4–e5. doi:10.1057/fr.2015.61, pp. 256, ISBN: 978-1-8490-5132-3 Jessica Kingsley Publishers, London

32. Felson, F. B. and Tedeschi, J. T. 1993. "Social Interactionist Perspectives on *Aggression and* Violence: An Introduction. In *Aggression and Violence: Social Interactionist Perspectives,* edited by F. B. Felson and J. T. Tedeschi, 1—10. Washington, DC: American Psychological Association. doi: 10.1037/10123-011.

33. Figueroa, J. P. 2008. "The HIV Epidemic in the Caribbean: Meeting the Challenges of Achieving Universal Access to Prevention, Treatment, and Care." *West Indian Medical Journal* 57 (3:): 195—203.

34. Fisher, B. S., Cullen, F. T., and Turner, M. G. 2000. "The Sexual Victimization of College Women." Report No. NCJ 182369. Washington, DC: Department of Justice. Available at https://www.ncjrs.gov/pdffiles1/nij/182369.pdf.

35. Gibbons. A.,(2015) *Family Violence in the Caribbean.* Presentation Expert Group Meeting on Family policy development: achievements and challenges United Nations Headquarters New York, 14-15 May 2015 *http://www.un.org/esa/socdev/family/docs/egm15/Gibbonspaper.pdf*

36. Gil, R. M. and Inoa-Vasquez, C. 1996, January 24. "Re: Marianismo: Origin and Meaning. " Online forum comment. Available at: userpages.umbc.edu/~korenman/wmst/marianismo.html.

37. Goetz, A. T., and Shackelford, T. K. 2006. "Sexual Coercion and Forced In-Pair Copulation as Sperm Competition Tactics in Humans. *Human Nature* 17 (3:): 265—82. Available at http://www.toddkshackelford.com/downloads/Goetz-Shackelford-HN-2006.pdf.

38. <u>Gong, J.</u>, <u>Stanton, B.</u>, <u>Lunn, S.</u>, <u>Deveaux, L.</u>, Li, X., Marshall, S., Braithwaite, N.V., Cottrell, L., Harris, C. Chen, X. 2009. "Effects through 24 Months of an HIV/AIDS Prevention Intervention Program Based on PMT Protection Motivation Theory among Preadolescents in the Bahamas. <u>*Pediatrics*</u> 123 (5 :): 917—28.

39. Groth, N. 1974. *Men Who Rape.* New York: Plenum Press.

40. Grych, J., and Swan, S. 2012. Toward a More Comprehensive Understanding of Interpersonal Violence: Introduction to the Special Issue on Interconnections among Different Types of Violence. *Psychology of Violence* 2 (2): 105–10. doi: <u>10.1037/a0027616</u>.

41. Gupta, G.R. 2001. *Integrating Gender into HIV/AIDS Programs.* Available at http://www.who.int/hiv/pub/prev_care/en/IntegratingGender.pdf.

42. Gupta, G., R. 2002. *Vulnerability and Resilience: Gender and HIV/AIDS in Latin America and the Caribbean.* Available at http://www.

unicef.org/barbados/spmapping/Implementation/HIV-AIDS/regional/
AIDS_Greta_Gender_2002.pdf.

43. Hamby, S., Finkelhor, D., and Turner, H. 2012. "Teen Dating Violence: Co-occurrence with Other Victimizations in the National Survey of Children's Exposure to Violence (NatSCEV)." *Psychology of Violence* 2 (2): 111–24. doi:10.1037/a0027191.

44. Hanson, R. K., and Morton-Bourgon, K. E. 2005. "The Characteristics of Persistent Sexual Offenders: A Meta-Analysis of Recidivism Studies." *Journal of Consulting and Clinical Psychology* 73 (6:): 1154–63. doi: 10.1037/0022-006X.73.6.1154.

45. *Healthy Relationships 2013*. Available at classroom.kidshealth.org/ 6to8personal/growing/healthy-realtionship.pdf.

46. Hylton, P. (2012). *The role of religion in Caribbean history*. CaribNation TV. https://www.youtube.com/watch?v=f-pTkUnb3v4

47. Iconis, R. 2008. Rape Myth Acceptance in College Students: A Literature Review. *Contemporary Issues in Education Research* 1 (2:): 47—51.

48. Jezzini, A. T., Guzmán, C. E. and Grayshield, L. March 2008. *Examining the Gender Role Concept of Marianismo and Its Relation to Acculturation in Mexican-American College Women*. Paper presented at the ACA Annual Conference and Exhibition. March 25-28 2008. Honolulu, Hawaii. Available at http://counselingoutfitters.com/vistas/ vistas08/Jezzini.htm.

49. Jouriles, E., Mueller, V., Rosenfield, D., McDonald, R., and Dodson, M. C. 2012. "Teens' Experiences of Harsh Parenting and Exposure to Severe Intimate Partner Violence: Adding Insult to Injury in Predicting

Teen Dating Violence. *Psychology of Violence* 2 (2:): 125—38. doi: 10.1037/a0027264.

50. Kahlor, L. and Morrison, D. 2007. "Television Viewing and Rape Myth Acceptance among College Women. *Sex Roles* 56: 729—39. Available at http://cultivationanalysisrtvf173.pbworks.com/f/RapeJS.pdf.

51. Knight, R. April 2011. "Preventing Rape: What the Research Tells." Keynote address at the 13th Annual MASOC/MATSA Conference. April 11-13, 2011Marlborough, Massachusetts

52. Knowles, V. H. 2008. *African Children Cry.* Nassau, Bahamas: One Rib Publications. ISBN 978156229010.

53. Knowles, V. H. 2016. a*frican children cry* (*2nd* ed.). Nassau, Bahamas: Unpublished manuscript. . africanchildrencry@gmail.com

54. Knowles, V., Kaljee, L., Deveaux, L., Lunn, S., Rolle, G., and Stanton, B. 2012. „National Implementation of an Evidence-Based HIV Prevention and Reproductive Health Program for Bahamian Youth." *International Electronic Journal of Health Education* 15:: 173—90. Available at http://www.aahperd.org/aahe/publications /iejhe/upload/evidence-based-HIV-prevention.pdf.

55. Koenig, L. J., Doll, L. S., O'Leary, A., Pequegnat, W., eds. 2005. *From Child Sexual Abuse to Adult Sexual Risk: Trauma, Revictimization, and Intervention.* Washington, DC: American Psychological Association.

56. Koss, M. P., Gidycz, C. A., and Wisniewski, N. 1987. "The Scope of Rape: Incidence and Prevalence of Sexual Aggression and Victimization in a National Sample of Higher Education Students. *Journal of Consulting and Clinical Psychology* 55 (2:): 162—70. doi:10.1037/0022-006X.55.2.162.

57. Lalumière, M. L., Harris, G. T., Quinsey, V. L., and Rice, M. E. 2005a. "Forced Copulation in the Animal Kingdom." In *The Causes of Rape: Understanding ID Individual Differences in Male Propensity for Sexual Aggression*, edited by M. L. Lalumière, G. T. Harris, V. L. Quinsey, and M. E. Rice, 31–58. Washington, DC: American Psychological Association. doi:<u>10.1037/10961-003</u>.

58. Lalumière, M. L., Harris, G. T., Quinsey, V. L., and Rice, M. E. 2005b. "Contextual and Situational Factors." In *The Causes of Rape: Understanding Individual Differences in Male Propensity for Sexual Aggression*, edited by M. L. Lalumière, G. T. Harris, V. L. Quinsey, and M. E. Rice, 143—57. Washington, DC: American Psychological Association. doi:<u>10.1037/10961-007</u>.

59. Latane, B., and Darley, J. 1969. Bystander Apathy." *American Scientist* 57: 244– –68. Available at http://faculty.babson.edu/krollag/org_site/soc_psych/latane_bystand.html.

60. Lee, <u>J. P.</u>, Jackson, <u>H. J.,</u> Pattison, <u>P.</u>, and Ward, <u>T.</u> 2002. Developmental risk Factors for Sexual Offending. <u>*Child Abuse & Neglect* 26 (1:</u>): 73–92.

61. Le Franc, E., Samms-Vaughn, M., Hambleton, I., Fox, K., and Brown, D. 2008. "Interpersonal Violence in Three Caribbean Countries: Barbados, Jamaica and Trinidad and Tobago.." *Pan-American Journal of Mental Health* 24 (6):): 409—21. Available at http://www.ncbi.nlm.nih.gov/pubmed/19178780.

62. Lisak, D., and Miller, P. M. 2002.. "Repeat Rape and Multiple Offending among "Undetected Rapists." *Violence and Victims* 17:73—84. Available at http://www.wcsap.org/sites/www.wcsap.org/files/uploads/webinars/SV%20on%20Campus/Repeat%20Rape.pdf.

63. Lonsway, K. A., and Fitzgerald, L. F. 1994. "Rape Myths: In Review." *Psychology of Women Quarterly* 18:: 133—64.

64. Lu S., (2015). White House taps psychologists to study sexual violence. *Monitor* February 2015, Vol. 46, No. 2 http://www.apa.org/monitor/2015/02/upfront-white-house.aspx

65. MACTS Center for Health Services Research. 2011. *Evidence-Based Multilevel Risk Reduction for Bahamian Mid-Adolescents.* Available at http://www.experts.scival.com/wayne/grantDetail.asp?t=ep1&id=9301475&o_id=123&.

66. Malamuth, N. M., and Check, J. V. 1984. "Debriefing effectiveness Following Exposure to Pornographic Rape Depictions." *The Journal of Sex Research* 20 (1:): 1—13.

67. WSDFSF, –McMahon, S., with Baker, K. 2011. "Changing Perceptions of Sexual Violence over Time."http://www.vawnet.org/Assoc_Files_VAWnet/AR_ChangingPerceptions.pdf.

68. Miller, L. E., Grabell, A., Thomas, A., Bermann, E., and Graham-Bermann, S. A. 2012. „The Associations between Community Violence, Television Violence, Intimate Partner Violence, Parent–Child Aggression, and Aggression in Sibling Relationships of a Sample of Preschoolers. *Psychology of Violence* 2 (2:): 165–78. doi: 10.1037/a0027254.

69. Mosenberg, D., ed. 2009. *Sexual and Gender-Based Violence in Africa.* Bulletin 83. Available at http://concernedafricascholars.org/bulletin/issue83-2/.

70. Muehlenhard, C. L., and Linton, M. A. 1987. "Date Rape and Sexual Aggression in Dating Situations: Incidence and Risk Factors." *Journal of CounselingPsychology*34(2:):186—96.doi:10.1037/0022-0167.34.2.186.

71. Mulliken, B. L. 2006. "Rape Myth Acceptance in College Students: The Influence of Gender, Racial and Religious Attitudes." *Dissertation Abstracts International: Section B: The Sciences and Engineering* 66 (11-B:): 62285.

72. Nagayama-Hall, G. C., and Hirschman, R. 1991. "Toward a Theory of Sexual Aggression: A Quadripartite Model." *Journal of Consulting and Clinical Psychology* 59 (5:): 662—69.

73. Neely-Smith, S. 2003. "The Influence of Self-Esteem and Self-Silencing on Self-Efficacy for Negotiating Safer Sex Behaviors in Urban Bahamian Women." *Dissertation Abstracts International* 64 (06-B:): 2594.

74. Nicolls, N. 2010. "Victims of Sexual Exploitation in the Bahamian Society: Adult "Men Exploiting Teenage Girls." Weblog message. Posted July 24. Available at http://caribbean-webcrat.blogspot.com/2010/07/bahamas-victims-of-exploitation-in.html.

75. Nunez, P. May 2007. "Bahamas Rape Count Shock." *BahamasB2B*. Available at http://www.bahamasb2b.com/news/story.php?title=Bahamas-Rape-Count-Shock.

76. O'Neil, M., and Morgan, P. 2010. *Perceptions of Sexual Violence: A Framework Research Report*. Available at http://www.frameworksinstitute.org/assets/files/PDF_sexualviolence/AmericanPerceptionsofSexualViolence.pdf.

77. Olive, V. 2012. "Sexual Assault against Women of Color." *Journal of Student Research*, 1: 1—9. Available at www.jofsr.com/index.php/path/article/download/27/19.

78. Padilla, M. 2007. *Fact Check. Available* at http://www.sph.umich.edu/news_events/findings/fall07/inFOCUS/five.htm.

79. PAHO (Pan American Health Organization); *Summary Report: Violence Against Women in Latin America and the Caribbean: a comparative analysis of population-based data from 12 countries.* Washington, DC: PAHO, 2013.

80. Pan Caribbean Partnership against HIV/AIDS ((PANCAP)). 2009. *Poverty and HIV/AIDS in the Caribbean: Final Report.* Available at http://www.pancap.org/docs/World_Bank_Studies/Poverty%20 and%20HIV%20Study%20Final%20Report%20-%20with%20 exec%20summary.pdf.

81. Payne, D. L., Lonsway, K. A, and Fitzgerald, L. F. 1998. "Rape Myth Acceptance: Exploration of Its structure and Its Measurement Using the Illinois Rape Myth Acceptance Scale." *Journal of Research in Personality* 33:: 27–68.

82. Pimorac, I. 1999 *Radical Feminism on Rape.* Available at hrcak.srce. hr/file/31856.

83. Quinsey, V. L., Skilling, T., Lalumiere, M. L., and Craig, W. M., 2005. *Juvenile Delinquency: Understanding the Original Individual Differences.* Washington, DC: American Psychological Association.

84. Reynolds, M. 2009. Report on the PCPress Conference to RRecognize the NDNational Day to ES VEnd Sexual Violence. Available at http:// crisiscentrebahamas.wordpress.com/2009/10/01/

85. Rico, N. 1996. Available at http://www.cepal.org/mujer/noticias/pagi-nas/9/27409/genderbasedvioilence.pdf

86. Rosenthal, D., and Peart, R. 1996. "The Rules of the Game: Teenagers Communicating about Sex." *Journal of Adolescence* 19:: 321–32. Available at http://firstcontent.oclc.org/ECOPDFS/ACADEMIC/ A1401971/A1904030.PDF.

87. Saedi, G. A. 2012.. "Movie Bad Boy = New Prince Charming? Is It true that Love Conquers All?" *Psychology Today. April 12 https:// www.psychologytoday.com/blog/millennial-media/201204/ movie-bad-boy-new-prince-charming*

88. Schwartz, B. K., and Henry, R. C., eds. 2006. *The Sexual Offender, Correction, Treatment and Legal practice*. Available at http://www. civicresearchinstitute.com /toc/TSO1_toc.pdf.

89. Schewe, P. A. 2002.. *The ICASA Scales: The Collaborative Development of Measures to Assess the Outcomes of Rape Prevention Programs in Illinois*. Unpublished manuscript.

90. Schewe, P. A., and Bennet, L. 2009. "Evaluating Prevention Programs: Challenges and Benefits of Measuring Outcomes." In *Preventing Violence in Relationships: Interventions across the Life Span*, edited by P. Schewe, ,247—61. Washington, DC: American Psychological Association.

91. Schuller, R., and Klippenstine, M. 2004. "The Impact of Complainant Sexual History Evidence on Jurors' Decisions: Considerations from a Psychological Perspective. *Psychology, Public Policy, and Law* 10 (3)) 321–42. doi: 10.1037/1076-8971.10.3.321.

92. Schwendinger, H., and Schwendinger, J. 1974. "Rape Myths in Legal, Theoretical, and Everyday Practice. *Crime and Social Justice* 1:: 18—26.

93. *Sexual Offences Act*. 2013. http://www.bahamas.gov.bs/wps/wcm/ connect/35889589-ab0b-4d65-ab17-e0fcd655f62a/Sexual+ Offences+(Amendment)+Bill,+2009+-+Justification.pdf?MOD=AJPE RESlOffencesandDomesticViolenceAct_1.pdf.

94. laws.**bahamas**.gov.bs/cms/en/**legislation**/index/by-category.html

95. Stromquist, N. P. 2007. *The Gender Socialization Process in Schools: A Cross-National Comparison.* Research Report No. 2008/ED/EFA/MRT/PI/71. Available at http://trylanarkcounty.com/wp-content/uploads/2011/09/Report-Gender-Socialization-in-Schools-Comparing-Countirs.pdf.

96. Thijs, A., and van den Akker, J., eds. 2009. *Curriculum in Development.* Available at http://www.slo.nl/downloads/2009/curriculum-in-development.pdf/.

97. Thompson, M. P., Swartout, K. M., and Koss, M. P. 2013.. Trajectories and predictors of sexually aggressive behaviors during emerging adulthood.

98. Psychology of Violence © 2012 American Psychological Association 2013, Vol. 3, No. 3, 247–259 https://www.apa.org/pubs/journals/features/vio-a0030624.pdf

99. Thornhill, R., and Palmer, C. 2000. *A Natural History of Rape: Biological Bases for Sexual Coercion.* Cambridge, MA: Massachusetts Institute of Technology.

100. Toronto, E. 1991. "The Feminine Unconscious and Psychoanalytic Theory." *Psychoanalytic Psychology* 5 (4) :: 415—38. http://psycnet.apa.org/journals/pap/8/4/415.pdf.

101. United States Agency for International Development [USAID]. 2009. *HIV/AIDS Health Profile: Latin America and the Caribbean.* Available at http://pdf.usaid.gov/pdf_docs/pdacu640.pdf.

102. UNDOC (United Nations Office on Drugs and Crime and the Latin America and the Caribbean Region of the World Bank). 2007. *Crime, Violence, and Development: Trends, Costs, and Policy Options in*

the Caribbean. Report No. 37820. Available at http://www.unodc. org/pdf/research/Cr_and_Vio_Car_E.pdf.

103. UNDP (United Nations Development Programme).2012. Human Development Report(UNDP Caribbean Human Development Report *http://caribbean.unwomen.org/en/our-work/ending-violence-against-women/advocacy-brief#sthash.wfEbKvDT.dpuf*

104. Valenzuela, T. March 2009. "Sex, Tourism and HIV." Available at http://www.poz.com/articles/sex_tourism_hiv_2303_16110.shtml.

105. Van den Akker J (2008) Curriculum development reinvented file:///C:/ Users/User/Downloads/Currdevelopment__re-invented.pdf

106. Ward, D., and Lee-Man, J. 2011. *The Handbook for Campus Safety and Security Reporting.* Washington, DC: US Department of Education: Office of Postsecondary Education. Available at http:// www2.ed.gov/admins/lead/safety/handbook.pdf.

107. Whitaker, J. D., and Lutzker, J. R., eds. 2009. *Preventing Partner Violence: Research and Evidence-Based Intervention Strategies.* Washington, DC: American Psychological Association.

108. Riguad, P. Implementing health and family life education (hfle) at a primary school in the north eastern education district in Trinidad and Tobago: teachers' concerns (2011) http://uwispace.sta.uwi. edu/dspace/bitstream/handle/2139/12710/Phyllis%20Rigaud. pdf?sequence=1

109. UNICEF (2009) Strengthening health and family life education in the region http://www.unicef.org/easterncaribbean/Final_HFLE.pdf

About the Author

D r. Valerie Knowles is a clinical child and adolescent psychologist, licensed by the Health Professions Council of the Bahamas. For more than twenty years, she has worked with high risk families in support of children and adolescents challenged with learning and behaviour problems. Dr. Knowles has served as the School Psychologist and Section Head of the Psychological Services Unit in the Ministry of Education; is the former Consultant Psychologist to the Bahamas' Ministry of Health and Social Development's local Juvenile Detention Centers; Past local Psychometric Consultant for the Inter-American Development Bank's Hopedale Project, (an executed grant that secured institutional strengthening and improved service delivery for persons with learning and behavioral challenges); past Executive Director of the Bahamas Family Planning Association; a former Clinical Director at Exodus Village (Male Drug Rehabilitation Centre; Bahamas Association of Social Health); former member of the Juvenile Panel in the Bahamas' Juvenile Court; Previous National Coordinator with the Implementation Fidelity Project (IFP) a collaborative research, HIV prevention effort between the Ministry of Education, the Ministry of Health, and Wayne State University via the Focus on Youth Project in the Bahamas; Invited Panelist at the United Nations' 49th Session of CEDAW held at the United Nations' Headquarters in New York; Member of the Bahamas Psychologist Association, American Psychologists Association, National Association of School Psychologist; Graduate of the traditional Government High School, College of the Bahamas, Elmira College,

New York; Completed Graduate Professional training with the Clinical Psychology Program in the Faculty of Medical Sciences University of the West Indies Mona Campus and the Northern Caribbean University both in Jamaica.

www.ingramcontent.com/pod-product-compliance
Lightning Source LLC
Chambersburg PA
CBHW072207280526
45788CB00002B/919